ANGKOR

An Essay on Art and Imperialism

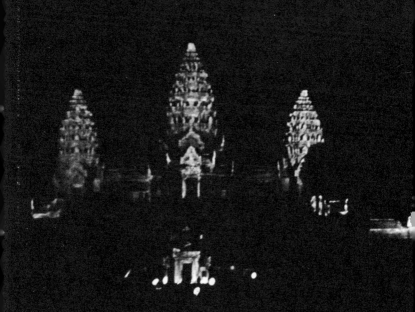

Also by Jan Myrdal

Report from a Chinese Village
Confessions of a Disloyal European

Also by Jan Myrdal and Gun Kessle

Chinese Journey
China: The Revolution Continued

JAN MYRDAL
and GUN KESSLE

ANGKOR

An Essay on Art and Imperialism

TRANSLATED FROM THE SWEDISH
BY PAUL BRITTEN AUSTIN

PANTHEON BOOKS
A Division of Random House, New York

Library of Congress Catalog Card Number: 74–90852
ISBN: 0-394-41516-7

Manufactured in the United States of America

FIRST AMERICAN EDITION

To Samdech Norodom Sihanouk

ANGKOR

An Essay on Art and Imperialism

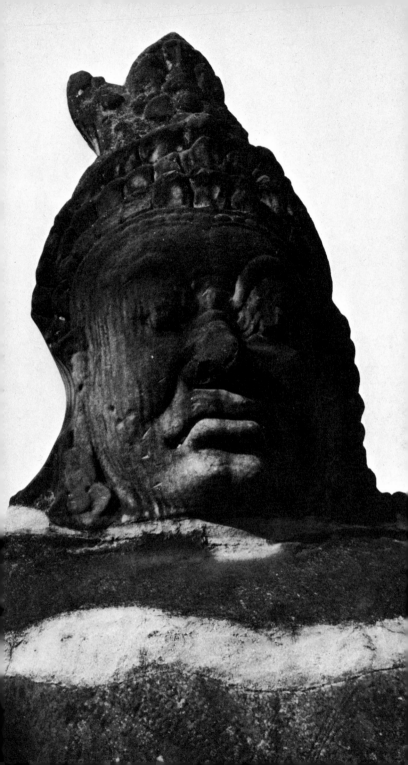

Face to Face

On February 22, 1967, the United States started the heaviest offensive of the war in Vietnam in "War Zone C." Over 25,000 troops were hurled against the Liberation Front. The operation began with the first combat parachute jump of the war. Troops were flown in by helicopter and deployed along the Cambodian border.

As heavy air and artillery bombardment was going on just across the border, Gun Kessle noted in her diary:

> 1.3.67
> 0700 quick breakfast, then Angkor Thom, South Gate; Bayon. Afternoon: Bayon reliefs. Hot.
> 2.3.67
> Started 0730. The Elephant Terrace, Preah Palilay. Afternoon: Bayon reliefs.
> 3.3.67
> My name-day. Left 0700 for Banteay Srei. Car stuck. Got lift with jeep.

Now, this can be interpreted as the normal petit-bourgeois intellectual attitude. At a time when villages are being burned down and people are fighting for their lives, at such a time intellectuals are strolling from monument to monument discussing the ornaments of the ninth century and the building techniques of the tenth century and a decline that took place eight centuries ago.

But this is not so. Both Gun and I—as other Swedish intellectuals—have taken a clear political stand on the war. Just before we left for Angkor and Cambodia, we had demonstrated, written articles, made speeches. Some months after we returned from Angkor, I was beaten up by the police and jailed after the big demonstrations in Stockholm. Later on, I was going to be charged with "inciting to rebellion" and threatened by a four-year jail sentence. But as the protest movement grew, the government backed down. In the end, some of the comrades were given shorter jail sentences, I and others got lighter fines only. The government did not want to create martyrs. Not at that time.

But this sounds like another typical intellectual attitude.

3

Demonstrating in the streets against the war, but working with "beauty and art." One day demonstrations and the next day an essay on Khmer art.

The war was going on just across the border; we were walking from monument to monument discussing ninth-century ornaments. That is true. But the discussion of ninth-century ornaments is also a part of the necessary struggle against imperialism.

This rotten society of ours is kept up by its dividing walls. Here a cell for revolt, there a cell for art; here a space for literature, there a space for economics—between them the walls. But these walls are load-bearing. The walls are the structure of this society. To raze them is a part of the struggle for liberation.

You stand face to face with the stone faces of Angkor. Beyond a border there is a war. But when you yourself face this stone then the "beauty" becomes a concrete reality. These faces of stone were hewn by sweating men in a bloody time of repression and revolt.

To write about Jayavarman VII and get beaten up by the cops; to stand in the midst of the dirt and violence writing fiction; to collect money for the striking mine-workers and

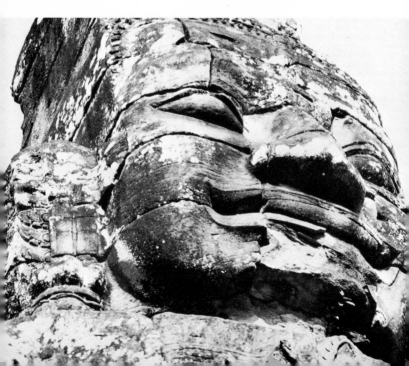

lecture on Strindberg; to publish the secret Swedish army regulations on the use of gas against "rioting" strikers and to demand back all of history and all the millennia—that is to take part in the razing of the load-bearing walls of imperialism.

To write on Angkor is a necessary part of the struggle for liberation.

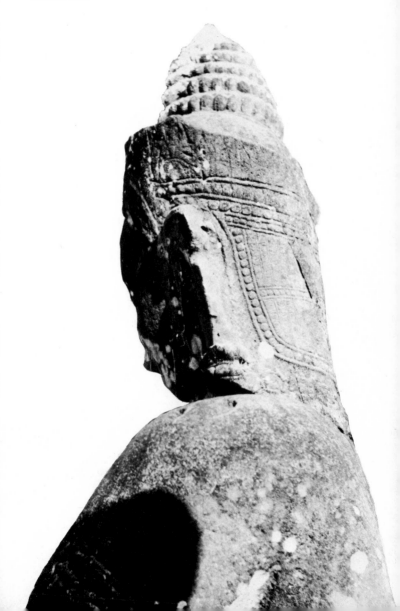

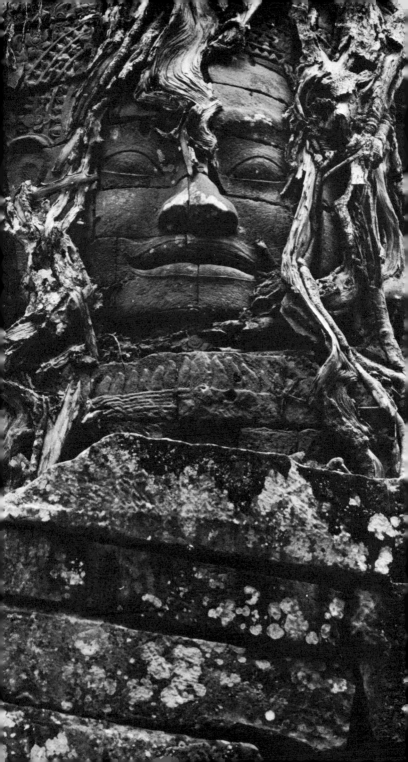

Ta Som (Ancestor Som) temple. Western gopura. Eastern façade. Sandstone from Phnom Kulen. Temple built in the reign of Jayavarman VII, late twelfth century. The face represents the Bodhisattva Lokesvara. It has probably been given the king's features. The roots are of a *Ficus religiosa* growing on the gopura.

Abandoned by his believers, entangled in the roots of the sacred pipal tree, Lokesvara, Lord of the World, the All-Seeing, stares out over the jungle. Soon eight centuries will have passed since the mighty ruler Jayavarman VII, restorer of the kingdom, ordered the construction of the temple and endowed the All-Seeing with his own features.

—The first is (probably) correct. But it is no answer. The second is full of beauty and thus lies. The third is necessary.
—What third?
—That which is based on the first, rejects the second, and takes a definite stand toward this face of stone.

Providence, heat, and monuments

It was hot. Somewhere up there in the darkness the ceiling fan squeaked and chirped. It was in March. We'd been in Cambodia one week. Now we were staying at the Hôtel de la Paix in Siemreap. A French provincial hotel, with a Chinese proprietor and Czech beer.

A lot of tourists had come to see Angkor. The better-off were staying at the Grand Hôtel d'Angkor or the Auberge Royale des Temples. The rich had taken whole suites in Villa Princière. Living an air-conditioned existence. By day they were to be seen among the temples; runny noses, bloodshot eyes.

Unused to this heat, I lie awake. Now I hear Gun's footstep on the tile floor. She's on her way to the shower. A plash of water. She snorts. As she comes back, I say:

"It's hot."

"Yes," says Gun. "Why, I wonder, has providence always arranged for great heat wherever the great monuments have been built?"

I went out to the shower. Didn't dry myself afterward. Just lay down all wet in my bed, letting the ceiling fan cool me off. I nearly froze.

"Pull the sheet over you, or you'll catch cold," Gun says.

"D'you hear the cicadas?" I ask.

"You promised to oil the fan," says Gun.

"How're your films getting on?" I ask.

"The real heat doesn't come until next month," says Gun.

I light a cigarette. It glows. In the dark I can't see the smoke, hardly feel I'm smoking. Stubbing it, I say:

"Apropos of providence . . ."

"Now you've woken me up again," says Gun.

". . . and heat . . ."

"Why can't you shut up! Just because you can't sleep, it doesn't mean everyone else has got to stay awake, does it?"

". . . and monuments . . ."

"Mohenjo Daro," Gun says. "Heat, huge rivers, and nitwits who can't stop talking at night."

I listened to the fan (which I should have oiled) and pondered the heat question.

Providence lets the heat blaze down where great monuments have been raised.

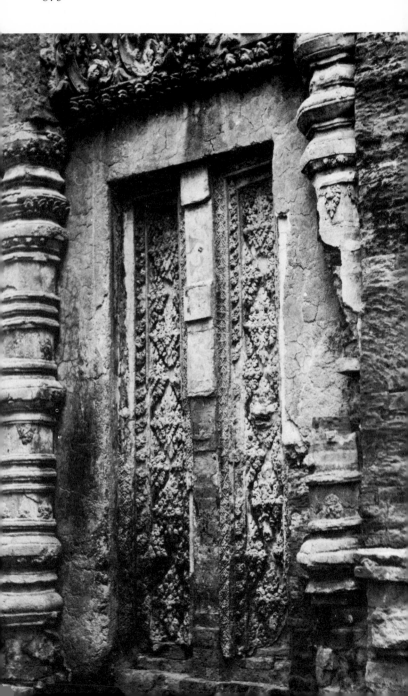

Brick with stucco decorations. King Indravarman I (877–889) had the six towers erected to house images of his parents and maternal grandparents; and of King Jayavarman II and his wife, in the shape of Siva and Devi.

Preah Ko belongs to the group of temples at Roluos, nine miles southeast of Angkor. There the founder of the Khmer Kingdom, Jayavarman II (802–850), had established his capital, Hariharalaya. Jayavarman II "gathered the soil together" and crushed the petty kings. In later ages, great men were to trace back their ancestry and their fiefs to his reign. Afterward Jayavarman had himself proclaimed king by the Brahmin Hiranyadama, so that the land of Cambodia should no longer be subject to Java and there should no longer be more than one king who was universal overlord.

In 877 Indravarman I succeeded to the throne and became god-king. He was declared to be a distant relative of Jayavarman II and of his son and successor Jayavarman III (850–877). Later on genealogies were drawn up to prove it.

If Jayavarman II founded the kingdom, Indravarman was its first master-builder. He began his reign by having the irrigation systems extended and ordering the construction of the great Indratataka dam, north of Hariharalaya, the capital. Preah Ko was the first great temple to be built.

*Theory and practice, or
the North German hen and Angkor*

Fifty years ago the geographer Ellsworth Huntington discovered that tropical peoples have narrow minds. There was a link between culture and temperature. In those parts of the world where the hottest month of the year has an average temperature not exceeding 60° F. and the coldest month an average not less than 38° F., culture flourished. From this it followed that the British climate was conducive to culture. London's was virtually ideal.

A few years later, in 1939, the great German professor of psychology Erich Jaensch, in his famous study of the differ-

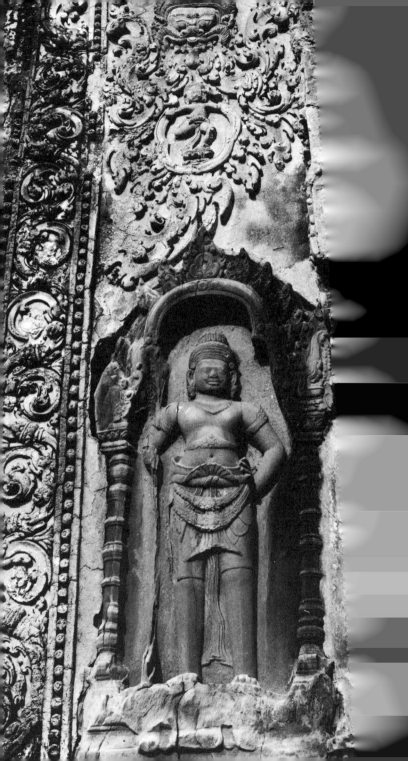

ences between northern and southern poultry, did pioneer work in developing similar ideas.

Since the differences, here demonstrated, as between the northern and southern types of human beings are also found in poultry and are also characteristic of the differences between the northern and southern hen . . . I believe we are in fact not guilty of any anthropomorphic error of interpretation of the factual relationships among our animals, if we describe the behavior of the northern hen as reliable in her reactions, purposive, and functional; in other words, if we attribute to the northern hen a certain disposition toward efficiency in her own field of activity, the hen-run.

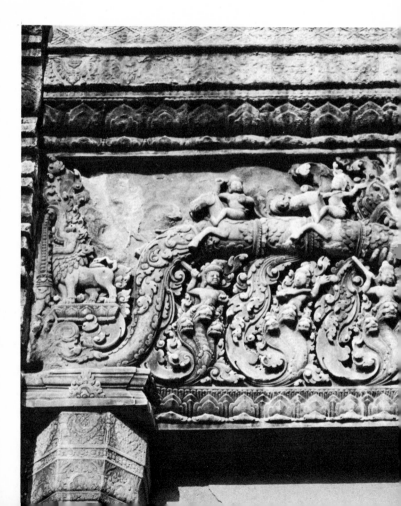

Angkor lies in Cambodia. Cambodia is tropical. Its climate is a tropical monsoon climate. Its temperatures are very far indeed from Huntington's ideal.

Here the average annual temperature is 80.6° F. April, the hottest month, has an average of 87° F. December is coolest, with 77° F. The lowest temperature to be recorded—at Phnom Penh—is 56° F. That chilly night occurred on December 1, 1955.

Between the maximum day and minimum night temperature there is a difference of 50° F. It reaches its peak between 12 noon and 3 p.m., is at its coolest between 2 a.m. and 5 p.m. In April the thermometer can rise to 104° F.

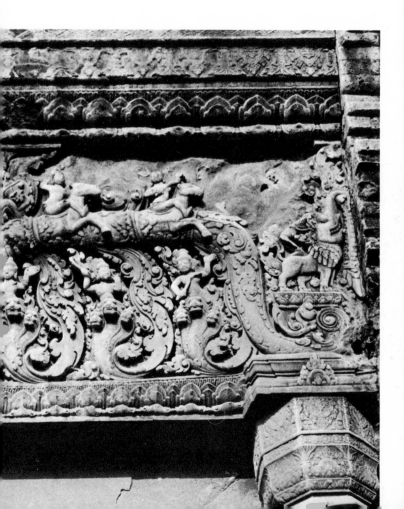

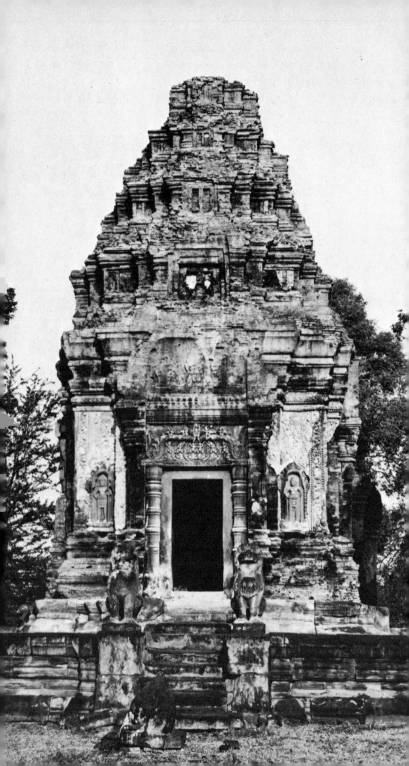

From May to November it rains. From December to April it doesn't. The annual rainfall is 59 inches. During the driest month—January—it is 0.25 inch. In the rainiest—September—11 inches.

Such are the climatic conditions. They affect the way of life. April, the hot, dry month before the monsoon rains, is a month of rest, a festive month—the month of the new year.

In the early hours of the afternoon everyone rests. Then the landscape is deserted. Men and beasts alike have withdrawn into the shade and are asleep.

Many tourists from Europe and North America, visiting Angkor, suffer from the heat. At Banteay Samre an English-woman says:

"How could people ever build anything in this heat?"

In his report from a visit to Angkor in 1296–1297, the Chinese diplomat Chou Ta-kouan, Kublai Khan's ambassador to King Srindravarman, writes of another sort of reaction to the Cambodian climate.

> Chinese sailors coming to the country note with pleasure that it is not necessary to wear clothes, and, since rice is easily had, women easily persuaded, houses easily run, furniture easily come by, and trade easily carried on, a great many sailors desert to take up permanent residence.

This is where the great monuments are. Here is a climate yielding a year-round growing season. And here tourists suffer from the heat. Maybe Jaensch is right? Maybe there *is* a difference, after all, between northern and southern poultry?

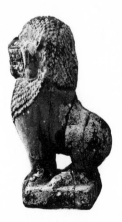

The temple mountain stands on a natural hillock. The first great sandstone edifice. Indravarman I himself calls it "a house of stone for Siva." It is possible that the work may have been put in hand even as early as the reign of Jayavarman II. The tower which crowns it is a later addition (c. 1150–1175).

The five stories of the temple rock are believed to symbolize the five levels of Meru, the Cosmic Mountain. The temple was devoted to the cult of the king—the divine Siva. The religious-architectonic expression of centralized authority.

Important to bear in mind, however, that we in point of fact know almost nothing about how the cults of this—or indeed of any other temple—functioned. Nor are we helped by comparisons with India; Khmer development was on quite different lines.

The reign of Indravarman II is regarded as having been peaceable. But—unlike his taciturn predecessors Jayavarman II and Jayavarman III—he left many inscriptions, thus reviving an older, pre-Angkor tradition.

During his reign, the Brahmins' influence was stabilized. As his spiritual leader, Indravarman had the Brahmin Sivasoma, a disciple of the South Indian philosopher Sankaracharya (c. 788–820). The latter, who may never really have existed, was not merely the restorer of orthodox Brahminism and an enemy of the Buddhists; in his fight against Buddhism, his doctrine—that only Brahma exists and that reality is illusion and ignorance—led him to exploit every popular fetish, every representation, and every image. Everything was only illusion anyway. Legend says that on his deathbed he prayed to the Almighty for forgiveness for having enclosed His infinity in stone and masonry. Whereafter he died and himself became an incarnation of Siva.

This was a religion suited to a ruler who owned all the soil, who called himself almighty, and who embodied a personal union with the divinity.

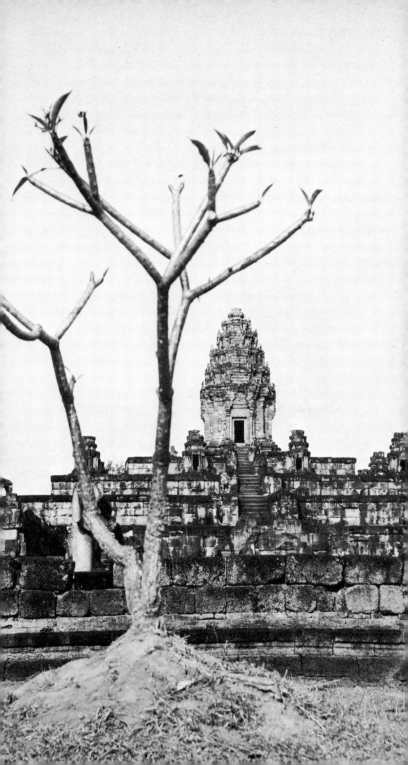

On killing a dog

All afternoon Gun has been photographing the reliefs at Bayon. Now we're sitting by the soft-drink stall in the shade of the trees, drinking Pepsi-Cola. We are sweating. We talk of the reliefs. An art historian has brooded over the Khmer artists' lack of perspective.

"Art historians theorize," says Gun. "It's because they've never had any practical experience of making pictures. It's all much simpler than they realize. These artists had been given the job of making clear, simple picture-stones, to be read from right to left. So they exploited the horizontal fields.

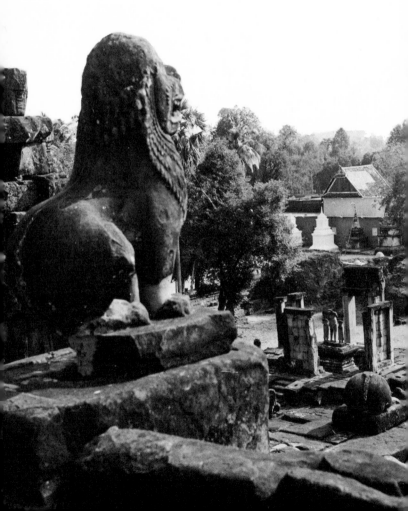

Down at the bottom, life on the shore. Up here, the lake. On the lake, battles between the Khmers and the Chams. It's simple. Easily legible. And clear. By taking a little pain they could have plotted out the whole thing in perspective. But then the cockfight in the foreground would have loomed larger than the battle in the background, and the course of events would have been hidden by branches and houses. The whole picture would have been screened in foliage and illegible."

We went on to discuss the pictorial sense. I got on to Professor Jaensch, the eidetic faculty, the doctrine of psychological types, and—finally—the question of the northern and southern hen.

"No," Gun said. "Even German tourists no longer dare mention his hen-yard theories. He was a Nazi, an anti-Semite. In order for a tourist to dare talk out loud about the purposiveness of the Nordic hen, he has to feel he has a more powerful army at his back than the one Germany possesses just now."

Well, she was right about that. No one any longer dares defend the superiority of the northern hen. On the other hand, the vast majority of tourists from Europe and North America go about imagining they're different from South Chinese and South Indians and Cambodians. Something they've learned in school. As a kid I read Carlson—Rönnholm—Moberg:

> French Indochina comprises the eastern part of Farther India. The inhabitants are Mongols, closely related to the Chinese, with whom they compete in willingness to work hard. For Europeans the climate is singularly unhealthy.

That was written in 1941. Nowadays no one raises his voice on this business of inhabitants being "prepared to work hard." Instead we talk about diseases and parasites that reduce their working capacity. The notion of Europeans being particularly sensitive to the heat, however, survives.

> The temperature is nearly 85° F. all year round. For a European the stifling air is hard to tolerate. (Forsström-Wennerberg, 1965).

19

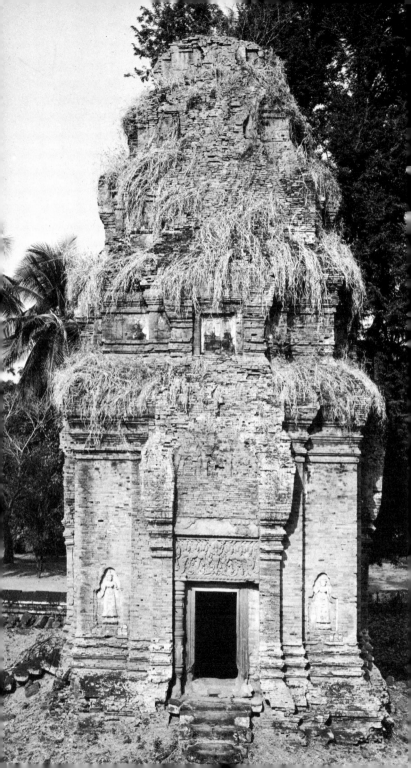

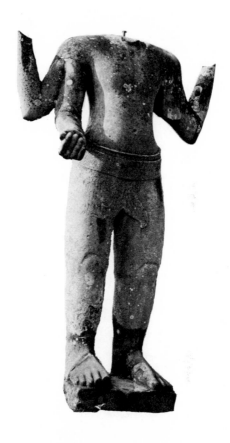

This is a truth to which each and every tourist in Angkor would subscribe. It is simple, normal; it corresponds to their experience. And therefore is true. And if it's true of people, then surely it must be true of poultry? Enter again (cackling), the Nordic hen. The purposive Nordic breed of poultry.

But this truth is just a trifle too self-evident. Against truths supported by well-tested experience and general opinion one always does well to deploy one's critical common sense.

For this truth, that "for a European, the stifling air is hard to tolerate," which every North American or European tourist

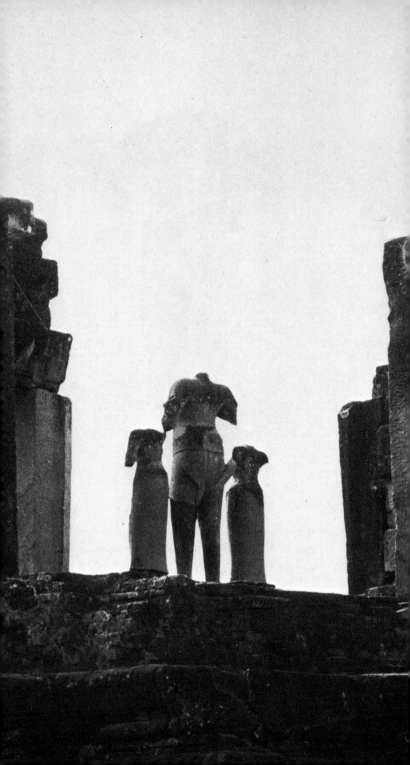

here at Angkor experiences in his own physique, accords only too well with the disorder currently prevailing in the world. It creates a certain illusion of order and meaning amid all the disorder and injustice.

White North Americans and Europeans live in cool countries. These cool countries have great industries, and that's where lies the economic power. Cool countries are well-developed countries.

Colored folk live in hot countries. These hot countries are economically underdeveloped. People there are poor.

= Culture develops in cool countries. (Huntington)

Europeans (white North Americans and Europeans, that is) find it hard to bear the climate in hot countries.

= Europeans are different

This way everything becomes so simple and obvious. The superior people have created a superior culture. The inferior have adapted themselves to an inferior existence. Those who carry culture on their backs have a duty to lead the world. Behind her wire netting the Nordic hen emits a purposeful cackle.

Beside us, where we sit sweating and drinking our Pepsi-Cola at the soft-drink stall north of Bayon, lies a dog. A short-haired, yellow-and-black street cur, not unlike a beagle. It is gasping for breath, in short, quick pants. Its mouth is open. Its tongue hangs out. Gun talks to the dog. It wags a friendly tail.

"We could take a German tourist who is suffering from the heat," I say, "lead him out into the sun, and march him round Bayon ten times. He'd sweat. But that's all. On the other hand, if we were to muzzle this dog and drag him out into the sun he wouldn't sweat. He'd die."

All over their bodies human beings have perspiratory glands. A dog hasn't. Human beings are better suited to the heat. And with respect to the number of perspiratory glands, no one, so far, has been able to detect any difference between "Europeans" and "non-Europeans." Here lies the crux of the matter.

The self-evident truth isn't true. That "for a European, the stifling heat is hard to tolerate" can be interpreted in social but not biological terms.

23

This name—Lolei—may be a latter-day echo of the name of the capital: Hariha*ralaya.* In type and function Lolei resembles Preah Ko. It was erected by Yasovarman I (889–c. 900) in memory of his father and predecessor, Indravarman I; also as a memorial to his mother, his father, and his maternal grandmother. It consists of four brick towers.

Yasovarman's mother, Indradevi, was descended from the old royal families of Vyadhapura, Sambhupura, and Aninditapura. This meant he restored pre-Angkor legitimacy. His spiritual leaders belonged to the Brahmin family on whom Jayavarman II had imposed the task of preserving the cult of the god-king.

Lolei was built on an island in the middle of the great dam Indravarman I had erected north of his capital. This dam was 4,155 yards long and 874 yards wide, and supplied both the capital and its surrounding agricultural lands with water.

Within the district today known as Angkor, Yasovarman I built a new capital, Yasodharapura, with its own temple-hill. He also had the great dam system, then known as Yasodharatataka, erected. It was 7,655 yards long and 1,986 yards wide.

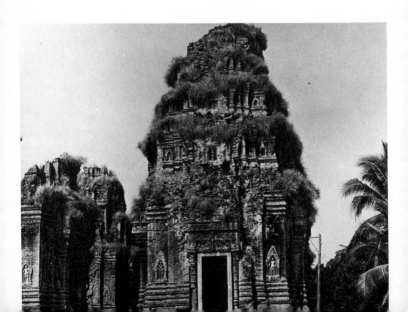

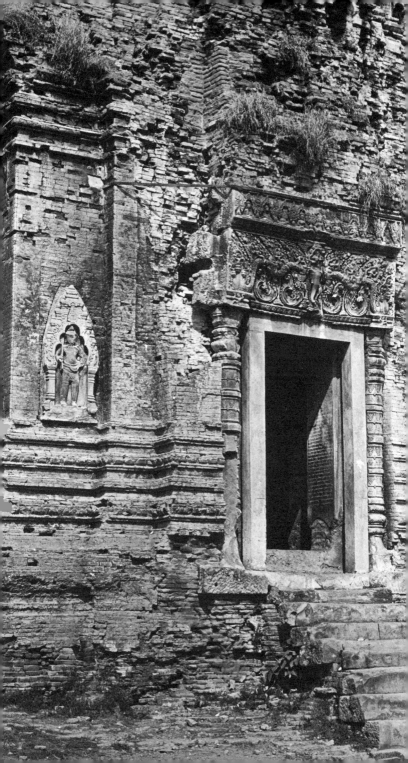

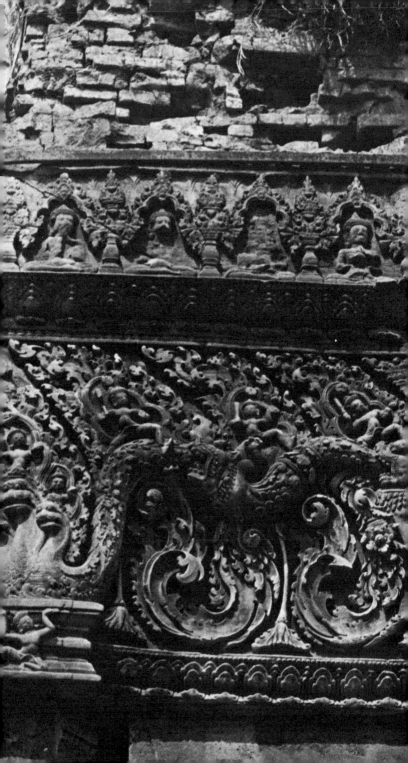

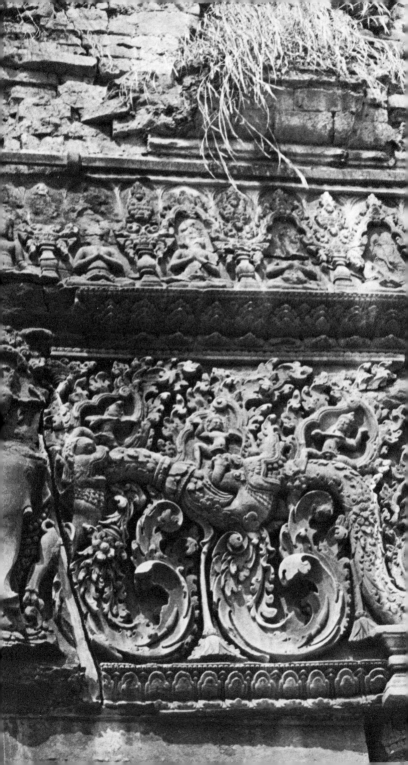

On the nature of illusory ideas

"Perspiratory glands!" exclaims my culture-bearing lady-reader. "Perspiratory glands, dribbling street curs, Pepsi-Cola, and Nordic poultry! What I wanted to read about was beauty. I want to understand Angkor. The majestic calm of the temples. The infinite perspectives of the architecture of Angkor Vat. Absorption into the All. The very essence, as it seems to us, of the impenetrable Oriental mentality."

"And what do you expect me to reply to that?"

"Quite simply—as long as you use her terminology there can be no understanding between you. Then reality is transformed into an impenetrable ideology. Just row upon row of words."

"Well and why not, if it makes her happy?"

"Because it also impoverishes her. She can collect beauty on her bookshelves and in her photo albums. She can wear her legs out walking round museums and gaping at monuments. None of this will change her. All she'll do is sink deeper and deeper into her own prejudices. And these prejudices serve a political function. So they must be unmasked—combatted, to help her see with new eyes; see and act. So—out of impenetrable ideologies and back to sweaty reality."

I write this one rainy morning in our Swedish province of Sörmland. It's cold. The air is hard to breathe. My muscles ache. My joints creak. All my old scars itch and tingle. Cursing this pissing Swedish climate of ours, I wish I was at Sind.

I'm not the only human being who's sensitive to the weather. But neither from my muscular aches and pains nor from my sensitivity to the weather do I draw any world-shaking conclusions. That I happen to find living in Göteborg insufferable doesn't mean Göteborg is generally insufferable, or that its climate is inimical to culture. Usually this distinction—between an individual's muscular aches and pains and the course of world history—isn't particularly hard to draw.

At the same time I do draw certain general conclusions from my aching muscles. They are a consequence of the drafty abodes of my youth; of damps, chills, and lack of warm, dry clothing. For this reason I'm interested in improved housing standards, so that others won't have to live in drafty, be-chimneyed rooms.

Where it's a question of suffering due to tropical climates, however, quite other conclusions—please note—are apt to be drawn. *Then* we fall to talking of diseases and parasites inimical to working capacity. Of malnutrition and poverty, which make life hard. We also stress the truism that in the tropics a sick, undernourished person, with parasites in his entrails, is more likely to feel poorly and to work less than a healthy, well-nourished person who has no parasites in his entrails—all quite irrespective of "race." In itself, and compared with the days when "natives" were said to be "lazy," this is progress.

But having said this, the textbook goes on:

> All this, in combination with the heat and humidity, inhibits the economy and standard of living. The tropical peoples are in high degree in need of the help which the UN and more fortunate countries can give them.
> (Forsström-Wennerberg, 1965)

And here the cloven hoof peeps out. Another quote:

> The original inhabitants of the jungle are food-gatherers, fishermen, and hunters. The heat, the humidity, and the profuse vegetation prevent them from raising themselves to a higher cultural level.
> (Forsström-Wennerberg, 1965)

Textbooks and reference books should be read with caution. They do not only transmit information; they systematize the accepted opinions of the prevailing system. Thereby, they often say more about the culture in which they are written than about the one they are describing.

In what concerns Göteborg, the textbook shares my view that my individual suffering from the Swedish west-coast climate lacks general import. While tropical heat, by contrast, does not:

(a) Europeans suffer more from heat than do natives.

(b) The climate, as such, hinders the natives from raising themselves to a higher cultural level.

(c) More fortunate countries must therefore help them to raise themselves to a higher cultural level.

Our discussion of perspiratory glands shows that "a" is wrong.

The existence of Angkor shows that "b" is wrong.

So what function, then, does "c" possess?

In our schools the Nordic hen cackles and cackles. These prejudices, implanted in our children, serve but one purpose: to justify the "Europeans'" economic power over "the colored peoples."

These prejudices can perfectly well be made to harmonize with talk about beauty, about Asia's soul, the impenetrability of the Oriental mentality, and Angkor's majestic calm.

So the prejudices must be combatted and rendered harmless. Then we can attend to the beauty.

EAST MEBON

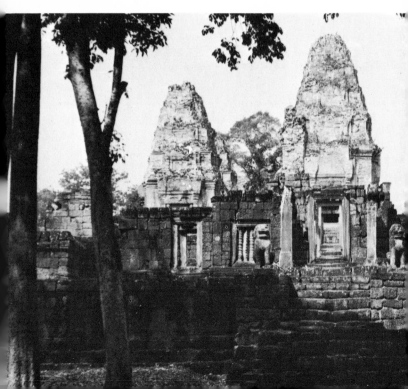

The Yasodharatataka irrigation dam's surface measured 4.8 square miles and it contained 52.3 million cubic yards of water. Rajendravarman (c. 944–968) had the East Mebon temple erected on an island in its middle. Its five temple towers are dedicated to the god-king and the memory of his parents, in the shape of Siva and Parvati.

A few years later, Rajendravarman had the Pre Rup temple erected on the south side of the irrigation dam. Dominating a rich agricultural plain, it was dedicated to his own royal divinity as Siva, to one of his ancestors on his mother's side as Vishnu, to his mother's sister as Uma, and to her son, his "half-brother," King Harshavarman II, in the form of Siva.

Rajendravarman had brought back the capital of the kingdom to the Angkor district. After Yasovarman's death, the latter had first been succeeded by his elder son, Harshavarman I (c. 900–c. 924), and, thereafter, by his younger son,

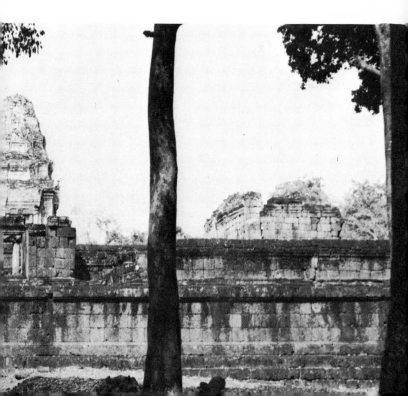

Isanavarman (c. 924–928). But while the latter was still on the throne, their maternal uncle had seized power and in 921 had caused the city of Yasodharapura to be abandoned; and taking with him the royal linga had erected a new capital, with new irrigation works and its own central temple, Koh Ker, fifty miles northeast of Yasodharapura. In 928 the maternal uncle became a legitimate ruler, Jayavarman IV (928–941). He was succeeded by his son, Harshavarman II (941–944) and after the latter's death—natural or otherwise—Rajendravarman acceded to the throne. He brought the capital back to Yasodharapura, "the sacred city which had long stood deserted," as the inscription puts it.

This apparently-involved family intrigue, in which the royal dignity zigzags about like a knight on a chessboard, is important; it makes it easier for us to understand the Khmer Kingdom and its history.

The legitimacy of Rajendravarman's title as universal overlord was based on the legitimacy of his maternal descent.

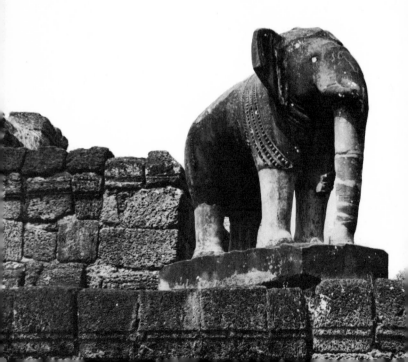

He was a nephew both of a sister of Yasovarman I and of a sister of Jayavarman IV. His mother was a daughter of Indravarman I, who on his mother's side was himself descended from old pre-Angkor royal families.

At the time when Rajendravarman describes his mother's sister's son as his half-brother, our own societies in Scandinavia were going through their most comprehensive and bloody revolution to date. The tribes, and their tribal society, were being crushed by the new aristocratic states; and in the *Völuspa*'s description of Ragnarök this is mirrored in the poetic crescendo from:

Brothers struggle and become each other's slayers

to

Sisters' sons tear asunder the bonds of kinship.

Rajendravarman's maternal cousin was a "brother," and this brother was no "usurper." This family chronicle, which, seen

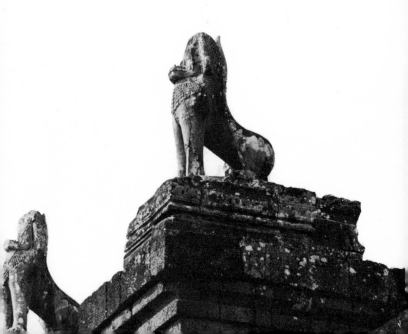

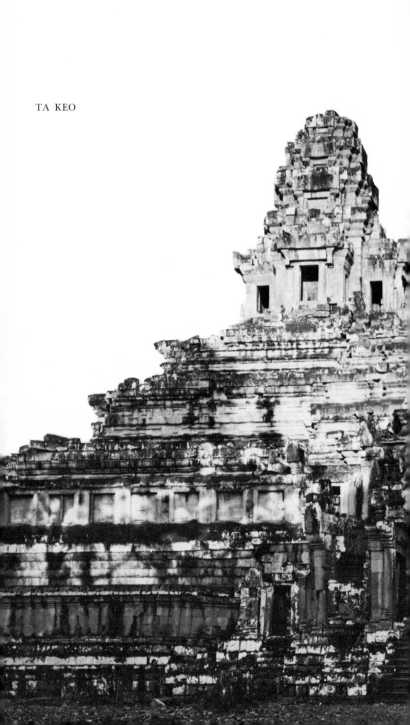

TA KEO

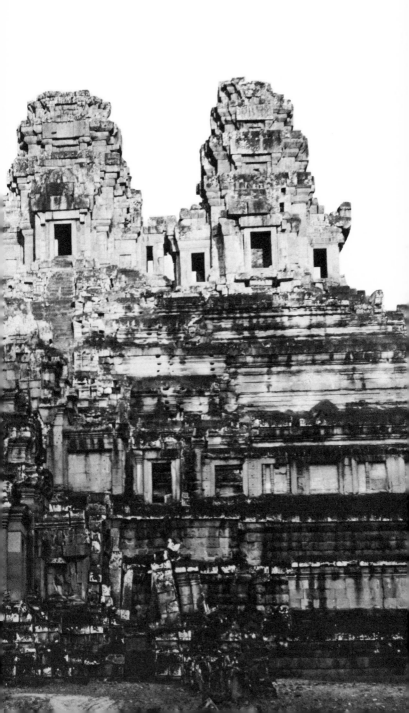

through latter-day patriarchal European eyes, seems so confused, becomes simple and natural enough according to the rules of a matrilineal society. The knight moves straightforwardly.

In taking the *Völuspa* as an example, I have two goals in mind. On the one hand, I want to underline the role played by matrilineal kinship in our own—Scandinavian—history. On the other hand, by being excessively explicit, I want to point out a dangerous mental trap.

The Khmer Kingdom had been converted to Hinduism. Its sacred language was Sanskrit. The Veda was its sacred writings. But Sanskrit isn't just any Indo-European language: it is that Indo-European language which during the nineteenth century was used as a basis for the theory of the existence of the Aryan peoples, their superior worth and natural right to rule over other peoples. Correlation of Rajendravarman with the *Völuspa,* and the role played in both cases by sisters' sons, could inveigle us into seeing the Khmer Kingdom as an expression of "Aryanism."

The theory of "the Aryan peoples" has been thoroughly exploded. But other notions persist, and the Hinduized Khmer culture tends to associate itself, via Sanskrit-Indo-European tongues, with "Europe."

But the lineage in the Khmer Kingdom, far from tying it to the India of the Vedas, clashes with the Vedantic world; Rajendravarman's inscription suggests the nature of its Hinduization. Vedantic India was patriarchal. The father was the head of the family. And his son was his heir. The daughter was subject to his authority and, after his death, to her brother's. To find inheritance systems where the sister's son is his uncle's heir we have to go to "non-Aryan" India. To southern India.

They possess certain points in common. But these common traits are older than Hinduization. Their history is open to discussion. But the sea was a bond of union. In Neolithic strata in Indonesia and Indochina, beads from India have been found. Common to the whole of this great monsoon-Asiatic area were irrigated rice-fields, tame buffaloes and oxen; a social organization, that is, high above that of "food-gatherers, fishermen, and hunters." On the ideological plane, the culture is reflected in cult-places on hillocks (later "temple mountains"), matrilineal inheritance, and ancestor-worship.

Rajendravarman's inscription, the political intrigues of the royal family, and the apotheosized ancestors all tie up with this.

It seems likely that Phimeanakas was begun as a central temple and temple mountain as early as the reign of Rajendravarman. It is the earliest example of vaulted masonry in Khmer architecture. Its galleries are roofed over. Phimeanakas, like Ta Keo, was probably built under Suryavarman I (c. 1001–1049). With a final comment on his accession to the throne we will leave these royal genealogies.

Jayavarman V (968–1001) succeeded his father Rajendravarman when he was still very young. During the first six years of his reign, he studied under his guru. Otherwise, little is known about his time. He was followed by a nine-year civil war between various pretenders to the throne, from which, in 1010, Suryavarman I emerged victorious. He asserted his descent from Indravarman's mother's side, and legitimized his royal status by marrying Viralakshmi, who descended from Yasovarman. Suryavarman's legitimacy was wholly matrilineal.

On the history of illusions

In 1555 and 1556, Gaspar da Cruz stayed in Cambodia. His account of the country was published in 1569. In it, he describes the religious and social state of affairs, tells of the difficulties he has encountered as a missionary, and says he has been ill. But on the heat he does not expatiate.

This is no mere chance omission. Sometimes one freezes. Sometimes one sweats. Sometimes the low pressure makes your shoulders ache. This is only human. But not until the latter half of the eighteenth century did "this stifling air" become "hard for a European to tolerate."

During the first centuries after Vasco da Gama's voyage, Europeans in South Asia were visitors, missionaries, soldiers.

They adopted customs as they found them. They dressed like other folk. Ate like them. Associated with them. They acquired wives and their wives gave birth to children, and the children were recognized as legitimate; and the Church looked benignly on these liaisons, which augmented the numbers of the faithful. So far, the Europeans were only an Asiatic people with a religion of their own. One people among many.

But their trade grew into empires. The empire-builders began to set themselves apart. They had become lords. They changed their eating habits. Acquired race-consciousness. In India, where the British had been victorious over their European rivals, they began to build their Empire. On March 14, 1786, officers' orphans dwelling in the Upper Children's Home in Calcutta were forbidden to go to Britain to study. In April, 1791, children with Indian mothers were excluded from employment in the East India Company's civil or military administration. In 1795 it was decreed that persons unable to prove they came both from a European father and a European mother could only be drummers, fife-players, musicians, and blacksmiths in the army. (Previously they had risen to be generals and commanders.) Such racism had a practical function: to legitimize the Empire and the exploitation of the country.

Clothes, too, changed. They became European and followed the European fashion. Since this grotesque idea flew in the face of common sense, it ran into resistance. Where argument failed, legislation was resorted to. As late as the 1830s, demands were still being made that the courts should intervene to get Europeans to abandon "native costume."

The stronger the colonial power became and the mightier the empires, the more elaborate the European tropical getup became. Sun helmets, puggarees, puttees—all served to underline the European's sensitivity to a tropical climate and his biological distance from "the natives." As a costume it was both impractical and physiologically absurd. But politically it was necessary. It was an ideological outfit. Only when the empires vanished did it vanish too. But then it vanished overnight, as if by magic.

But neither this costume's ideological character nor its

insult to common sense prevented it from having a physiological effect. Man is an adaptable animal. His body has a highly developed, built-in heat regulator. A human being can perfectly well carry out hard physical labor in extreme heat. He sweats.

But European clothing and European tropical getup change the conditions for this built-in heat regulator. Perspiration increases, and the sweat which is exuded by clothed skin contains twice as much salt as sweat exuded by skin that is naked to the air. This has nothing at all to do with race. It is just as valid for colored people as for uncolored.

Thus arose the state of affairs which, wherever Anglo-Saxons, Frenchmen, Dutchmen, and Belgians ruled in the tropics, came to be regarded as normal. The rulers went about dressed up, and the ruled undressed. The rulers suffered from the colonial syndrome (now known as the aid-to-developing-countries syndrome): irritability, lethargy, inability to do any physical labor, and incapacity to persist in any intellectual effort, depressions and delusions of persecution; in extreme cases, even cramp, i.e., deficiency of salt.

But this very suffering, which disqualified Europeans from doing anything but administrative and bureaucratic work, was regarded by the Europeans themselves as proof positive of their own biological superiority. And this too is why, in the Anglo-Saxon culture, the notion developed that Portuguese, Spaniards, and other Latin peoples were biologically inferior, were "colored." For the lower classes of these latter peoples had been transported out to the tropical colonies and there been put to hard physical labor. Their very ability to do it was taken by the British as evidence of inferiority.

The statement I find in my Swedish textbook, that "for a European the stifling air is hard to tolerate" has behind it a very clear political and social history.

The European clothing was functional: it served to preserve society. Nor, in fulfilling this function, was it specifically European. In order to demonstrate its own superiority, the ruling class renders itself physiologically incapable of doing any work. In his *Diary of an East Indian Journey,*

Pehr Osbeck, the pupil of Linnaeus, describes the clothes worn in Canton in 1751:

> No one is allowed to dress above his station . . . In winter they are capable of wearing thirteen or fourteen coats, one above the other, or lined with fur, and, instead of a muff, they carry a quail in their hand. The poor have to make do with a little short coat of blue cotton, long sailors' trousers, and raincoats of bamboo leaves. They go barefooted and more often than not are naked to the waist . . . Laborers must cut their nails, while superior persons let them grow as long as they can, keep them perfectly white and transparent, and at nights preserve them in bamboo sheaths.

The Chinese diplomat Chou Ta-kouan, who visited Angkor at the close of the thirteenth century, reacted in exactly the same way as educated Europeans were to do in later ages. He pointed out that the climate was insufferably hot. He

PHIMEANAKAS

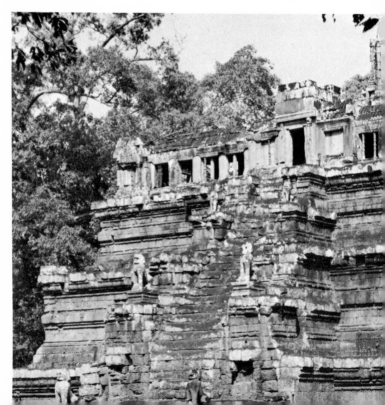

also remarked on the natives' deficient clothing, the frequency with which they bathed, and on their loose morals.

This "European" illusion isn't European; it's a matter of class. It also explains the way in which the human figure is depicted at Angkor. Demons, slaves, "common folk," all have muscles; they experience feelings, show passions, and carry out work. Gods, kings, and apsarases (the heavenly dancers), on the other hand, are characterized by their "elevation of spirit," by their calm, peace, "all-seeingness," and a pneumatic physique. Their bodies have not been physically developed. They've been inflated.

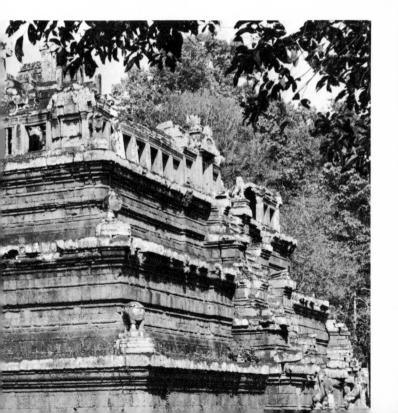

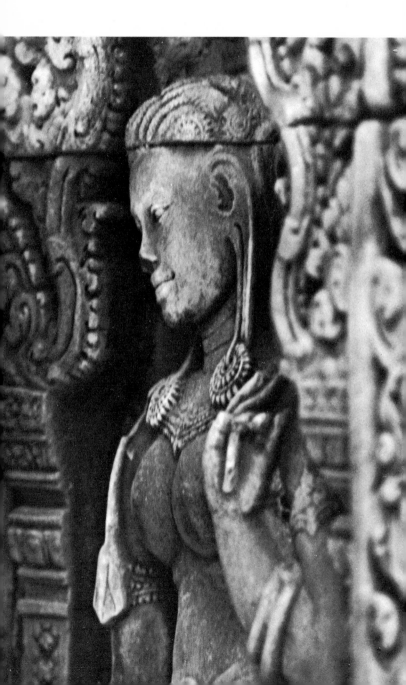

In the middle of the forest, far from all other monuments, twelve miles northeast of Angkor, lies Banteay Srei. It is built of hard, pinkish sandstone. A little temple, for which only the best—and, at Angkor, rare—stone has been used. The artists have also fully exploited the materials. Of all the Angkor group of temples, it is agreed, Banteay Srei is both the most opulent and the one which forms the most complete and harmonious whole. It is also virtually the only one ever to have been completed.

This is the temple which André Malraux plundered in December, 1923. Using stonemason's saws and chisels, he hacked out six cornerstones with apsarases and "several ornamental reliefs." Just before midnight, on Christmas Eve, 1923, he was arrested on board the river steamer while on his way to Phnom Penh with his booty. The stolen goods were impounded. Afterward, at his trial, Malraux defended himself by asserting that the monument was not one of those which were "protected." After a while the case was dropped. But Malraux was never acquitted. When Banteay Srei was restored in 1924, the stolen goods were brought back from the museum warehouse at Phnom Penh and replaced in the temple wall.

That Banteay Srei wasn't "protected" was a super-subtle and legalistic defense: Lieutenant Marec, of the colonial power's "École Française d'Extrême-Orient," whose business it was to study, describe, and maintain the monuments, sent an architect, by name Georges Demasur, to measure and photograph the temple. Unfortunately he died before completing his task, leaving the measuring to be finished in 1916 by the head of the archaeological department of EFEO, the famous Henri Parmentier. Parmentier took Banteay Srei as his starting point for a new view of the various periods of Khmer art. Owing to war conditions, however, his report—containing four pages of photos and three drawings—was not printed in the *EFEO Bulletin* until some years later. It was this report which André Malraux had read in the Bibliothèque Nationale in Paris. Having done so, he set off for Cambodia to satisfy his love of art, collect sculptures, and repair his own finances.

Later in the trial, the lawyer asserted that, since Banteay Srei had only been described scientifically and was not mentioned as a "protected monument" in any juridically valid decree, it was to be regarded as *"res derelictae"*—an ownerless object.

That Malraux was young and foolish is one thing. That the colonial authorities exploited his theft politically is self-evident. What is less self-evident is why the intellectual left wing in France should have backed Malraux up. André Breton said it was absurb to send someone to prison for raping two or three stone dancers. This radical support for Malraux concealed a profound, if hidden, chauvinistic scorn for culture. Would they have rallied to the defense of a young Cambodian poet who got himself arrested for collecting stone figures in the Parthenon to repair *his* finances?

Banteay Srei is one of the temples whose dating has long been in dispute. It has presented a choice of several inscriptions. The temple's flowery wealth of ornament gives an impression of being in a late "Gothic," "flamboyant" style; and it is true, one inscription is to be found dating Banteay Srei at 1304, in which case it must have been built by King Srindravarman's (1295–1307) teachers and relations. So, for example, says Benjamin Rowland, in the Pelican History of Art Series (1953). This would make the temple the last great peak in classical Khmer art.

But in 1936 an inscription—dating from 968—concerning the temple's foundation was discovered. Specifying the positions of the sun, the moon, and the planets, this yielded April/May, 967, as the date. In that case the temple would have been founded by Jayavarman V's guru Yajnavaraha and his younger brother. It is this dating which has subsequently been generally accepted.

This question of dates is not marginal. For if the temple is to be placed in the fourteenth century, then we must change our view of the Khmer Kingdom's last period. Banteay Srei would witness to a final decadent flowering. In that case, the religious and social conflicts of that age would acquire another character; the temple would have been built twenty-three years before Cambodia's last Sanskrit inscription and

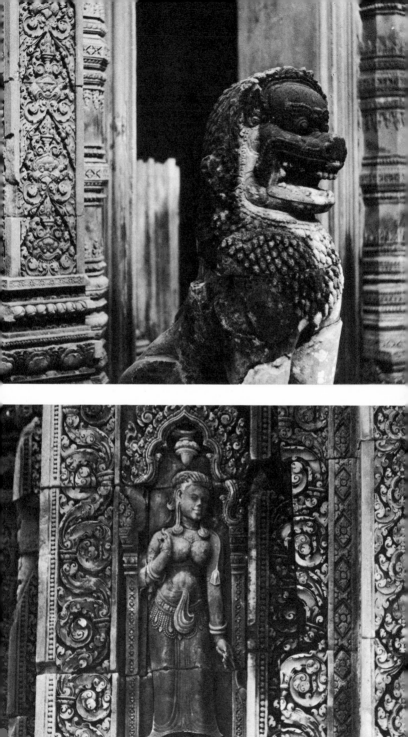

would be an expression of the Sivaistic reaction that followed after Jayavarman VII, and be an index of its strength even at that late date.

That it should have proved so problematic to place this richly ornamented temple in its proper context in art history may seem strange. But for a long while, the whole question of the dating of Khmer art remained confused. It is an art which seemed to have grown up within the course of a few centuries, as if Lolei and Bayon had been built simultaneously. Not until Philippe Stern looked into this problem in 1927 (in *Le Bayon d'Angkor et l'évolution de l'art Khmer*) did a chronology become possible. Which also made it possible to trace the history of the Khmer Kingdom.

But Banteay Srei is particularly problematic, since its sculptures are intentionally archaic. Whether the temple's

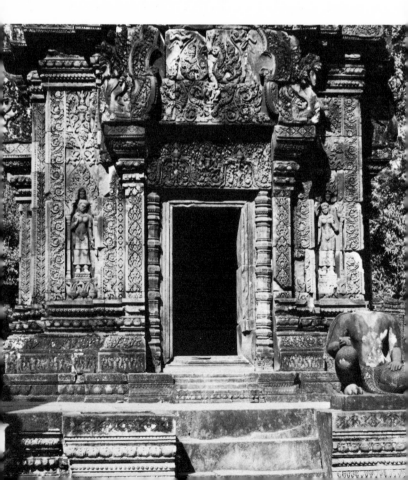

construction is placed in the tenth century or the fourteenth, its archaicizing style is unmistakable. Nor is Banteay Srei a royal temple. The figures of its relief talk to each other. They discuss. They live. The apsarases stand in their niches, soft and pliable; and even if their costumes and hairstyles point back to past centuries, their faces are new, alive. All chill, all majesty, has vanished. It is a neat and pretty art.

And while the reliefs on the door lintels clearly reveal their relatedness to Mamallapuram—the Dravidic temples of southern India—and their artistic tradition, Banteay Srei is something wholly new.

In all India it has no counterpart. Its architectural wholeness, the details of its ornament, the smiles on the faces of the apsarases are both in the Pallava tradition and entirely foreign to it. Many Indologists have placed these temples in "Greater India." But this is an optical illusion. One might equally well say—and some have—that India forms part of "Greater Greece."

The sandstone at Banteay Srei has not been cut. It has been carved. It has been carved like wood. This is timber

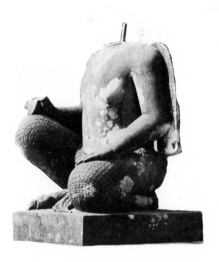

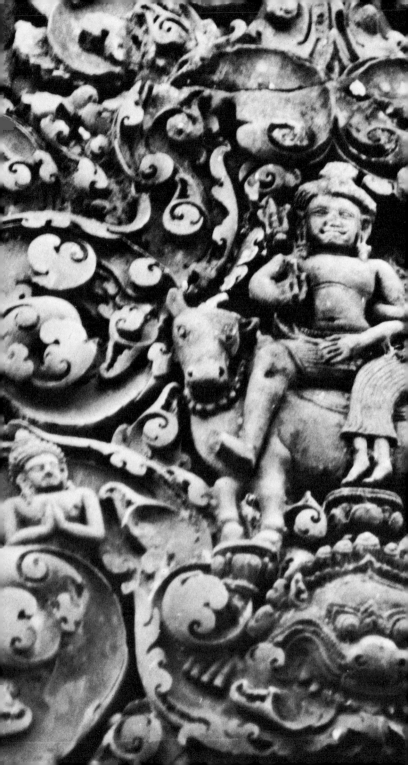

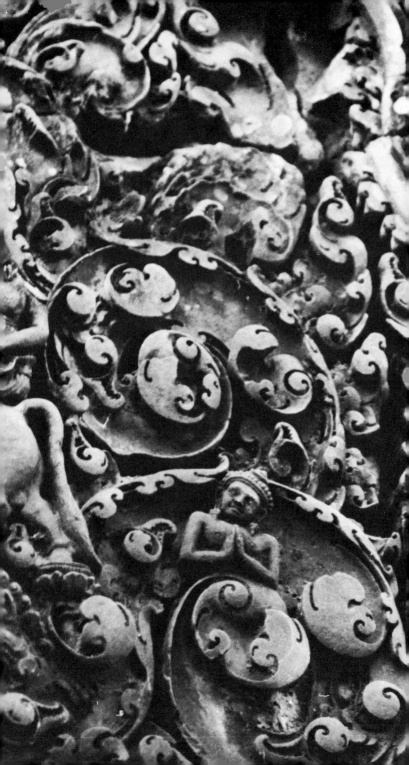

architecture in stone. The stone's fine quality permitted it to be treated in this way. And with this observation vanishes our last possibility of dating Banteay Srei to the fourteenth century.

In the neighborhood of Angkor good stone was then in short supply. Normal architecture was timber architecture. Dwellings and palaces had all vanished long ago. Temples were built first of timber, then in brick. Not, however, with mortar, but with a vegetable "glue" which made the joints almost invisible. (A technique still used in India and Vietnam.) Sandstone was precious material. But the quarries were soon emptied of good stone. Later artists and architects had to adapt to poorer grades. Banteay Srei represents the peak of this sandstone art. It is the only building wholly executed in sandstone. Sandstone was used later, too, but by the end of the reign of Jayavarman VII the seams were exhausted.

But Banteay Srei has something else to tell us. Hitherto we've spoken of "universal overlords." But Banteay Srei was not built for a king. It was built for a Brahmin, a high aristocrat. Nor is it the only temple of its kind. The realm was being administered by the aristocracy. And this makes its history more concrete for us.

For this neat, pretty, "artistic" temple too had its great irrigation dam.

—Who built Angkor?   —Who discovered Angkor?

— *Alexander the Great!!*   — *France!!*

World trade was considerable. In the ports of China, Arabs jostled with Persians, with Javanese skippers and seamen from Ceylon. Toward the mid-thirteenth century the inspector of foreign trade at Fukien, Chau Ju-kua, noted in his survey of trade with foreign countries, that communications between China and Cambodia had been established in 618–627 and that Cambodia had sent her first ambassador to the "present" dynasty in 1120.

Fifty years later the great standard Chinese work on Cambodia was written: customs, mores, economy, Angkor's architecture, etc. Three centuries later—at the period, that is, when we teach our schoolchildren the world was first discovered—the first description of Angkor to be published in Europe saw the light of day. The book was printed in Barcelona in 1601. In it, the Franciscan friar Ribadeneyra states that many people thought Angkor had been built by Alexander the Great or by the Romans.

It's true that the struggle between Jesuits and Dominicans in the mission field yielded no practical results in terms of conversions. But one thing it did achieve. It gave rise to a vast literature. Filling entire libraries, this literature in turn had, at least, one good result: China became known in Europe. As Voltaire points out, it was more thoroughly described than many a European province.

One of the more readable—and, in its day, widely read—of these contributions was the Dominican Navarrete's *Tratados históricos* . . . (Madrid, 1676). He writes:

> I did not mention Camboxa to this purpose, tho I am not sorry it came into my mind; my design was to give an account that [at Angkor] sixty Leagues up the River [Mekong] beyond the Court [Udong] there are certain beautiful Buildings, with the most curious Workmanship imaginable; the Relation of their Excellency and Perfection which was brought to Manila astonish'd all Men. I sent that which I had from Don Francis Enriquez de Losada into Spain as a Rarity, there is no inserting of it in this

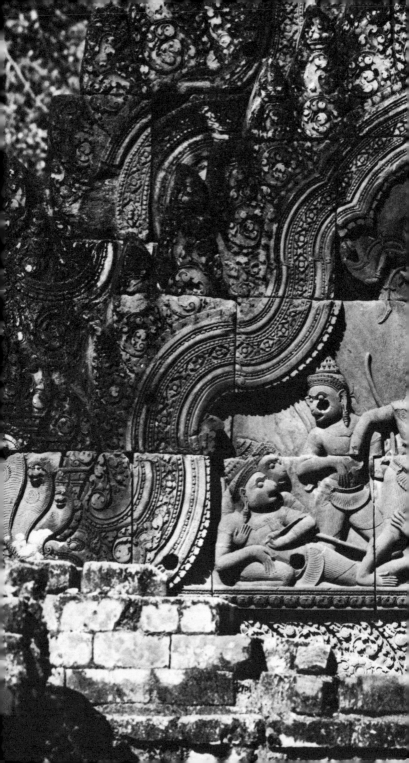

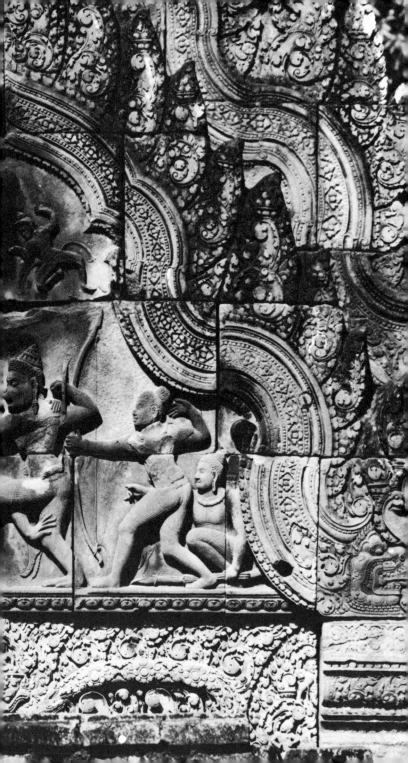

place. The Work, some say, was done by the Jews, others that it is Roman: Some will have it to be the Work of Alexander the Great, who they fancy travelled thus far, and order'd that stately Palace to be built as a Memorial to Posterity of his being there. It consists of Square Courts and Cloisters, as they are in fashion at present, but no part is without fine Mouldings and Carvings, it is the Aranjuez of those Kings. When Don James de Losada went over thither to build the Ship I said was cast away, the King [Ramadhipati; 1642–1658] was there taking his Pleasure, and therefore the Spaniards went up thither and saw this Wonder.

In 1604 another Spanish monk, Gabriel Quiroga de San Antonio, had given more detailed information as to the identity of the builders of Angkor:

This habit . . . has reached them from the Roman Jews, who formerly lived in this kingdom. There are many Jews in the kingdom of China; and it was they who built the city of Angkor in Cambodia, a city which, as I have said, was discovered in 1570.

To complete this picture of European astigmatism it suffices to look up the word "Angkor" in Meyer's *Neues Lexikon,* 1961, and let it express an officially socialist European view of the matter:

. . . The ruins of the temples (A. Vat) from the 12th c., and the palace (A. Thom) with the important Bayon Temple from the late 9th c., were discovered by French archaeologists in 1860 . . .

But . . . Angkor was built neither by Alexander the Great, nor by Roman Jews. Angkor was built by the Cambodians. Nor was it ever "forgotten." As late as 1577, Angkor Vat was restored by Satha I. Its inscriptions preserve the names of kings and master-builders. No "mystery" here!

We should know more about Angkor if the Cambodian state archives had not been burned in 1594, when Thailand troops took the city of Lovak. But this catastrophe was also a consequence of the dirty game being played by Portuguese

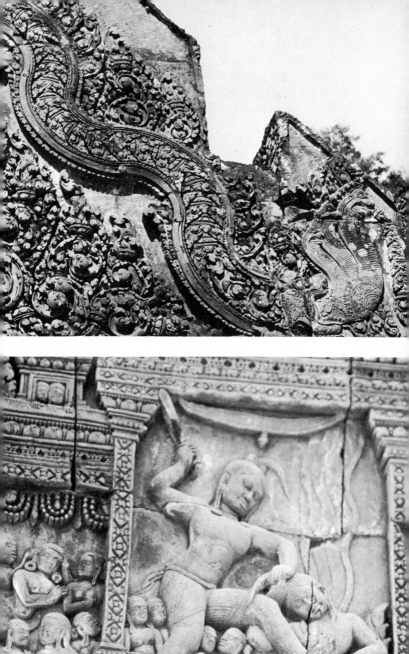

conquerors and the Dominican monks surrounding Satha I.

During the last century, French archaeologists have done great work. But they have never claimed to have "discovered" Angkor. Indeed, they have had so little success in disseminating what they know that European mystery-mongers can still tell lies without fear of being caught out. In Europe we still feel perfectly free to talk of "the age of discovery" and the "unknown kings" who built the city of Angkor, over which hovers the "enigma of the East."

Thommanon
c. 1100–1150

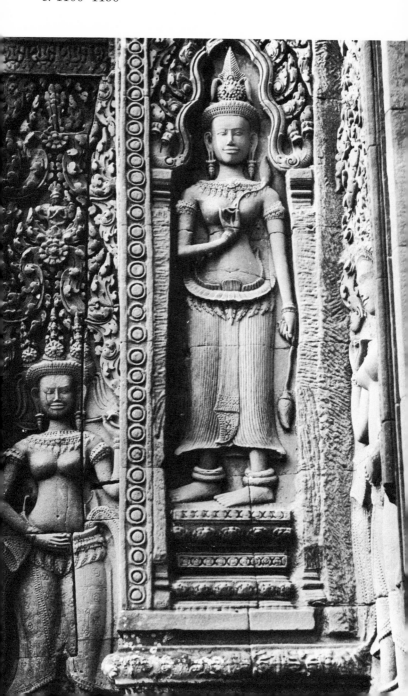

In the reign of Suryavarman I the Khmer Kingdom expanded. At the same time the aristocracy greatly increased its power. Agricultural output rose as a result of the cultivation of great areas west of Lake Tonle Sap. This soil either belonged to the new temples or had been enfeoffed to aristocrats.

Suryavarman was a Buddhist. But this made no difference to the official cult of the royal divinity. The power of the Brahmins grew. From the leading Brahmin family, Suryavarman elevated the young Sadasiva, giving him his wife's sister to wife (and it was on the maternal side, it should be remembered, that Suryavarman himself asserted his own legitimacy). It was Sadasiva who, in the king's name, had to carry out the work of building the temples.

On Suryavarman I's death, Sadasiva had Udayadityavarman II (1050–1066) proclaimed king. Udayadityavarman gave Sadasiva a royal title. The Brahmin ruled through the king. An immense new dam system was created—a system which, even if partly choked with slime, functions to this very day. It measured 8,748 by 2,405 yards = 6.7 square miles. A new capital was also built.

In 1051, the first serious revolt broke out. It was crushed by General Sangrama. In 1065, two more serious rebellions were put down by the same general. In 1066, Udayadityavarman II was succeeded by his younger brother, Harshavarman III (1066–1080).

But the dissolution of the kingdom proceeds. The monarch can no longer recover his power over the provincial lords, whose power is steadily growing. The king's armies are defeated in battles against Champa. His alliance with China against Tonkin proves to be a failure; the Chinese offensive against Hanoi turns out badly, and the Khmer armies are routed.

The Brahmin Divakarapandita abandons Harshavarman III and supports one of the lords of the northern provinces. In 1080, though this potentate is in no way related to the families which hitherto have reigned, the Brahmin Divakarapandita crowns this potentate king. In return, Jayavarman VI (1080–1107) accords the Brahmin royal titles. This king's power, however, does not seem to have reached as far as Angkor; and when, in 1107, he dies, the Brahmin Diva-karapandita crowns his elder—and, according to the inscriptions, reluctant—brother: Dharanindravarman I (1107–1112).

At this time there seem to have been two monarchs in the kingdom: at Angkor, a successor to Harshavarman III appears to have held sway. But in 1112 the son of Dharanindravarman I, who "was still very young and had just concluded his studies," rebelled. In 1113 he was crowned King Suryavarman II (1113–c. 1150) by the same Brahmin Diva-karapandita.

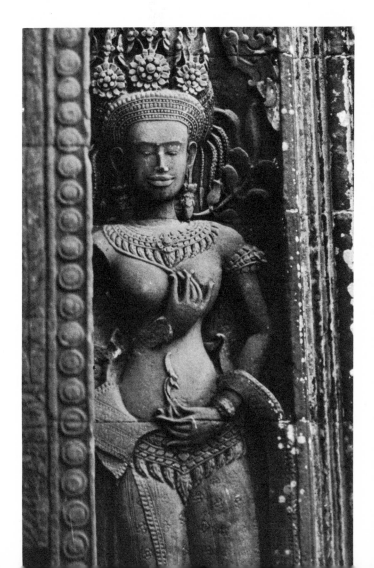

Angkor Vat
c. 1100–1150

Suryavarman II, who had begun his reign by ordering the death of his predecessor—or by killing him himself—became a great conqueror. He was always at war. Again and again he sent ambassadors to China. In 1128 the Chinese Emperor recognized him as a grand vassal, and trade was regulated. Suryavarman had Angkor Vat built as a mausoleum temple for himself, as Vishnu. It is one of the world's great stone buildings.

His death is shrouded in obscurity. His last inscription dates from 1145. Yet it seems likely the attack on Tonkin, in 1145, was ordered by him. For the armies of Khmer, it was a disaster.

Angkor Vat was never abandoned. It remained a temple and, through all the wars and changes of religion, a goal for pilgrimages. This temple was—and is—a national symbol.

The bas-reliefs at Angkor Vat cover a surface of about 13,990 square feet. They were the first of their kind at Angkor. According to many art critics, they are also—even if different parts of the reliefs have been executed at different times, in different styles, and are of varying quality—the most splendid. They are religious. Their motifs are Vishnavistic. In these pictures Suryavarman II identifies himself with Vishnu.

The Angkor reliefs seem to leap ready-made into existence. There is nothing haphazard about the tympanums at Banteay Srei. They bear witness to a pictorial tradition. But so do the immense monumental reliefs at Angkor have roots in the past. Yet there seems to be nothing earlier to find. But these reliefs are three-dimensional paintings. Only a few traces of Angkor's ancient paintings survive. All others have been destroyed by the climate. It was a mural painting tradition these reliefs consummated.

The design of the reliefs was then determined by the structural form. In Angkor Vat the relief is about a half-inch deep. It is on the inner wall of the galleries. Protected against the direct sunlight; at the same time bathed in reflected light.

When the temple was built, the ceiling of the galleries—according to Chinese sources—was covered with Chinese silk. In Banteay Srei the reliefs stand in direct sunlight. There the artists could model them with light and shade.

But maybe not just the other way around

It is possible to trace influences of Hellenistic art in Angkor.

There is also a striking resemblance to the Italian Renaissance in the decorative art of Angkor.

For the Hellenistic influences it is possible to establish a chronology. The dates will jump from the West eastward on the map.

But for the Italian Renaissance it is different; the ornaments appear several centuries earlier in Angkor than in Italy.

The likely attitude in our schools when confronted with this is that it is found "normal" for Hellenism to influence eastward (trade, Alexander, the Greco-Buddhist kingdoms). But the fact that the ornaments of Angkor predate those of Renaissance Italy tends to be interpreted as a coincidence.

But from 1300 A.D. onward, Chinese, Asiatic motifs are being utilized in European silk-weaving. They are either directly copied or blended with traditional European and Byzantine patterns.

There are many other examples. The "coincidence" becomes "normal." To face Angkor is also to face—and in facing distinctly see and interpret—the attitude of the "cultured classes" of Europe and North America. It is not a coincidence that they find it "natural" for Hellenism to spread eastward and "coincidental" (or of minor interest) that the Angkor ornaments predate the Italian Renaissance.

Such "first thoughts" and "natural" responses are suspect. When you put the spotlight on them, you can distinctly see them for what they are:

Both lower varieties of our species, the black and the yellow races, constitute the crude raw material, the cotton and the wool, which the various branches of the white

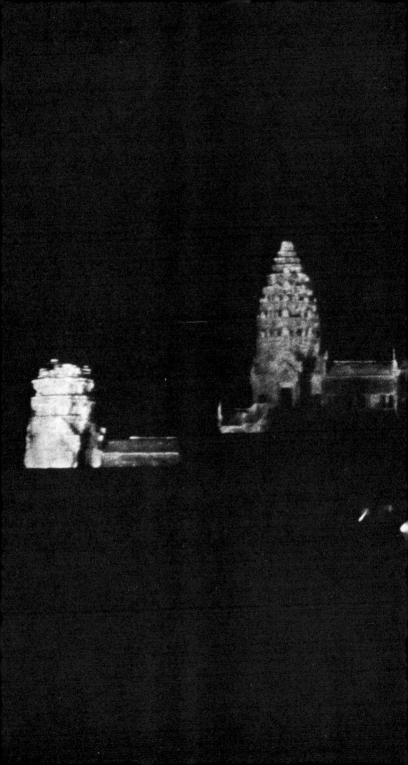

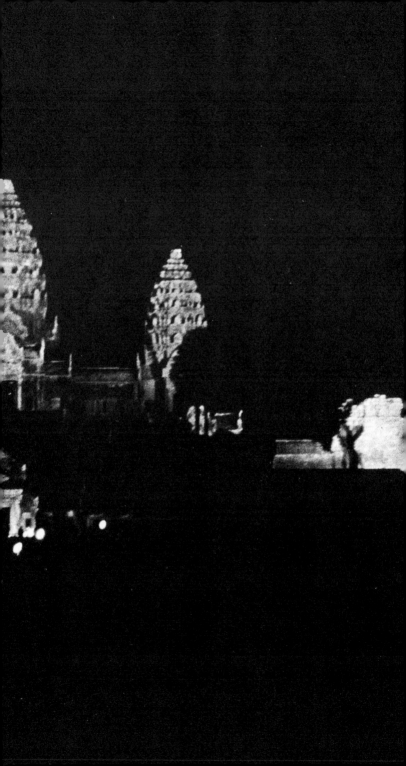

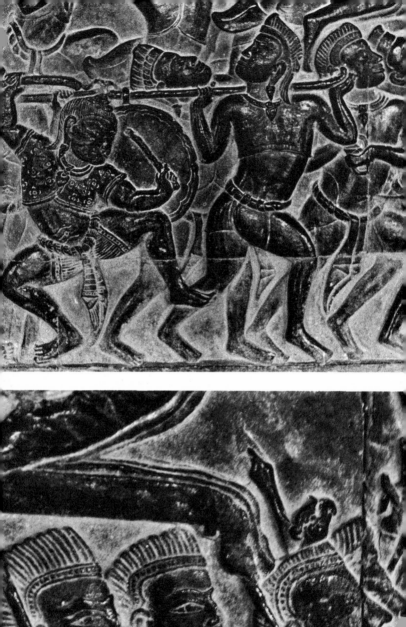

race soften with its silk, while the Aryan group spins its fine thread through the refined races showing its silvery and golden arabesques as a blinding masterpiece upon their surface.

Count Gobineau wrote this in the last volume of the work in which he tried to prove that all great things (including the high culture of South America) have been the work of Aryans.

Exposed to light—it bursts. It is unscientific. It is spurious. After Gobineau came Chamberlain. And after him, Hitler.

The year 1855 was the year in which Livingstone reached the Victoria Falls. Gobineau may not have been writing about Angkor, but he was expressing colonialism's thoughts, the thoughts of European Empire. He was formulating the ideology urgently needed by Europe's rulers.

And that's why the way our cultured classes react, when faced with the question whether the Italian Renaissance had any roots in Angkor, is by no means unimportant. And why there's nothing funny about the ease with which one can always find a public for such statements as that bearded "white men" founded the higher South American cultures.

To face Angkor and admit what one sees, then, implies a liberation from the dangerous myths of European superiority. For ideas are dangerous. They condition action. Now the villages are burning. Napalm can't be washed away. Behind the war which the rulers of the United States are waging on the villages lie economic and political motives. But also ideological ones. Reality is always overdetermined. And that's why the ideologies, too, must be crumbled to pieces: and why to ask oneself why one found it "absurd" that Angkor should have influenced the Italian Renaissance is to pose a serious question.

Nor can we elude the matter by reversing our reactions. "Asia" that influenced "Europe." Very good. But one can also dig up just as many—and just as tenable—proofs (for example) of Hellenism's influence on Asia. The thing has been done. But to deny a myth is not the same as to escape from it. To deny is to affirm.

Where is Angkor? In Southeast Asia! Quite right. But this is a vast area. The term does not identify. Well then, where *is*

Angkor? In Indochina. Yes, it lies between India and China. It traded with both India and China. At Angkor glazed brick was used, which means a Chinese influence. At Angkor there were Brahmins, which means India. But words seduce ideas. Words make our evaluations for us. Behind the expression "Indochina" lurks the notion that Angkor was "a bastard culture."

Where, then, does Angkor really lie? In Farther India. Or, as certain art historians call it: "Indian Asia." Or, as others, "Greater India."

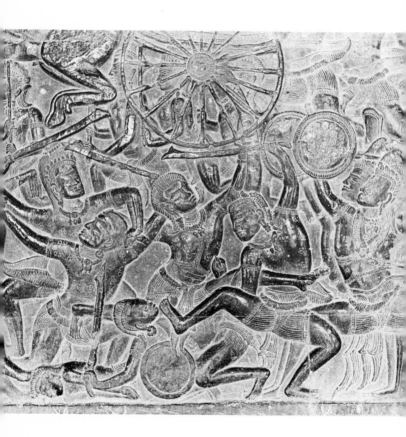

Look at Angkor! Hellenistic? Yes! Indian? Yes! Chinese? Yes! But Angkor, its art, its culture, cannot be expressed in some such formula as:

$$\text{Angkor} = \text{X Indian (Hellenistic) Y} \frac{\text{Chinese}}{\text{Javanese}}$$

Angkor is Sanskrit, *nagara,* a word meaning city or town. The city had many names but was always known as Angkor, "the city" (town). People in this city spoke the same tongue as

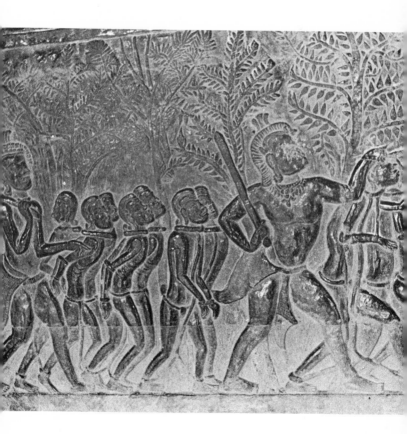

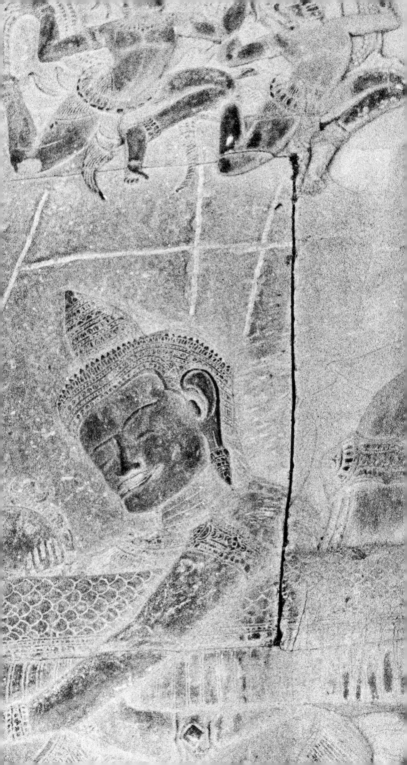

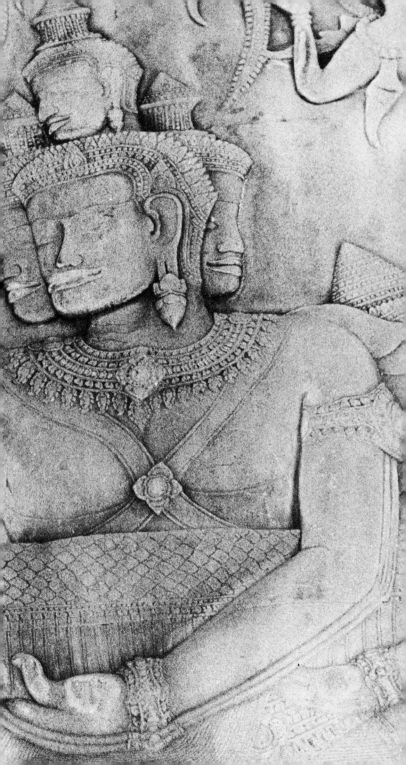

their forefathers and the same tongue as their descendants. Khmer. Angkor lies in Cambodia.

To see and accept Angkor is to admit the dual truth that Angkor's art both exerted and submitted to influences and that the art of Angkor is the art of Cambodia.

Angkor is unique. The world is manifold.

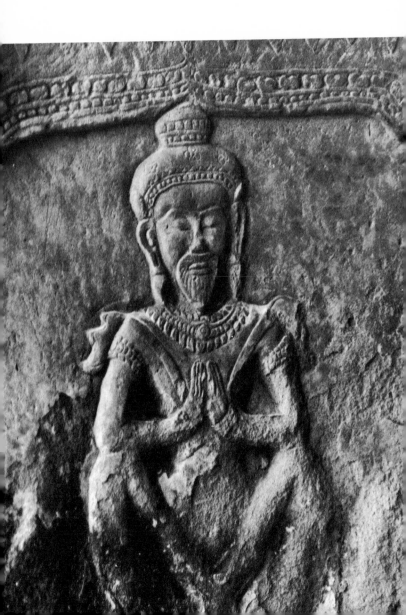

Banteay Samre

c. 1100–1170

Suryavarman's empire had been a mighty one. Contemporary Chinese chroniclers had noted its expansion. But toward the mid-twelfth century its provinces begin to behave like independent kingdoms. By then Suryavarman has vanished from the throne. No inscription tells us when or how. He has been succeeded by Dharanindravarman II (c. 1150–

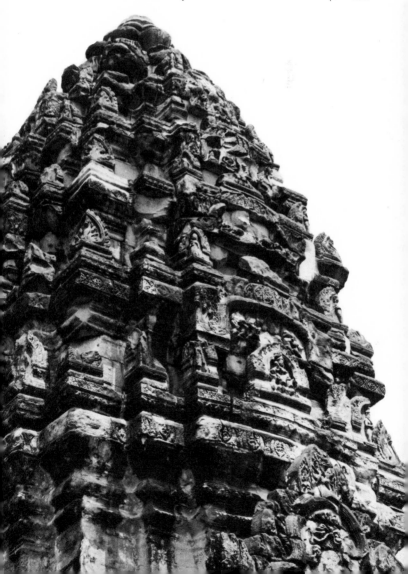

1160), the son of his maternal uncle. The latter is married to a daughter of Harshavarman III and by her has a son who one generation later will make himself famous as Jayavarman VII. Legitimacy still goes by the distaff side.

Dharanindravarman II breaks with orthodox tradition. He is a Buddhist. Riots and revolts, wars and civil wars follow one another. After the death of Dharanindravarman, the prince, who is later to become Jayavarman VII, fights on the losing side in a civil war against a highly placed official who, in the year 1165, kills Yasovarman II. The usurper is crowned king, under the name of Tribhuvanadityavarman (1165–1177). The war against Champa goes on. In the end, Champa's fleet forces its way up the Mekong and into Tonle Sap. On the fifteenth day of the fifth month of 1177, Angkor is taken, the usurper is killed, and the city plundered. The Khmer Kingdom becomes an occupied country.

North of the lake

From the air one can see old irrigation canals. But as one drives down along the road north of the lake, one sees savanna. Occasional agricultural areas, second-rate forest lands. Here, north of the lake, the soil is not much good. This is no wealthy region. Population density is low. In the fertile agricultural regions of Java and in North Vietnam, population density can be as high as 772 per square mile. Here, a hundred years ago, it was around 4 to 8 persons per square mile. Today it is said to have risen to 27 persons per square mile. Only 14 percent of the soil is cultivated.

Yet a thousand years ago this was a wealthy, fertile land. Perhaps 1,000,000 people were at work here. This was the basis of a kingdom, an empire. From here, armies set off for the wars, here great temples were built. But now it's a poor corner of the country. Its soil is poor. But not destroyed. Two thousand years ago it was just as poor as today. What happened, then, eleven hundred years ago, to create all that wealth?

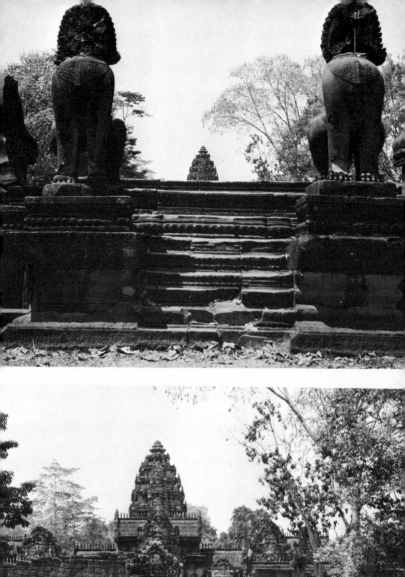
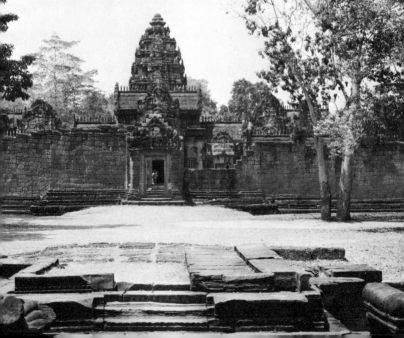

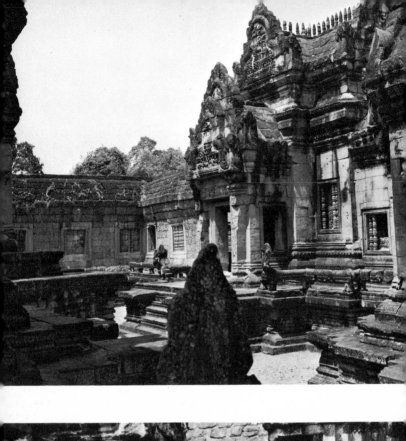

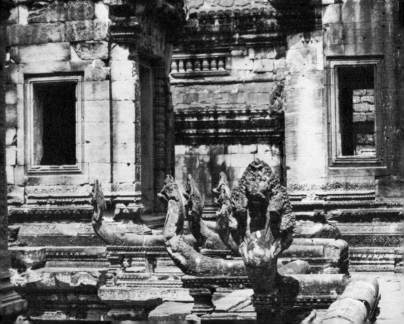

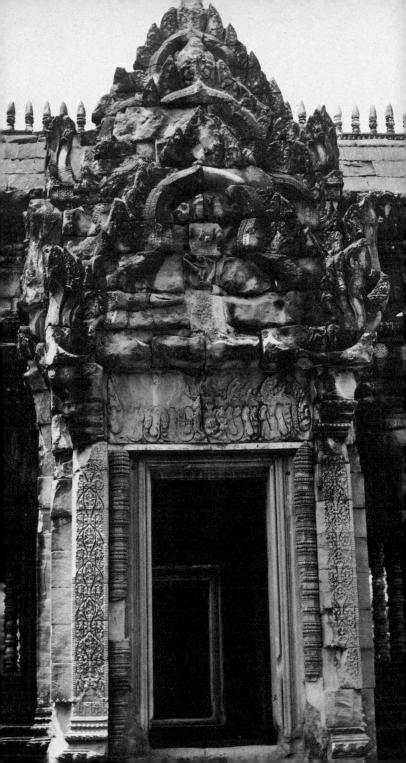

The climate is hard. Drought seasons, rainy seasons. At low water, the Siemreap River flows at the rate of 35 cubic feet per second, has a maximum depth of 10 feet; and in March, the Mekong River rises at the rate of 1308 cubic yards per second, until one day in mid-June the tide turns and the waters of the Mekong River flow into Tonle Sap. The lake rises, flooding the plain. Tonle Sap becomes a lake of 3860 square miles, with a maximum depth of 8 fathoms. During the first days of October, the tide turns again. For 255 days in the year, the water flows from Tonle Sap into the Mekong. For 10 days a year there is no current. For 100 days the water flows from the Mekong into Tonle Sap.

Fishing in Tonle Sap yields 100,000 tons of fish a year. That means wealth. Fish consumption stands at 51 pounds per head of population per annum. Forty thousand people live by fishing.

This is and was the framework. Fishing, irrigated agriculture on poor soil. Floods and burning and clearing. What happened north of the lake eleven hundred years ago was a technological revolution. A new type of irrigational agriculture made it possible to exploit the soil north of the highest water-level. This technological revolution shattered the old society, tore down its property laws, and created a new state, a new religion, and a new ruling class.

The new irrigation system multiplied the crops and produced an enormous surplus, but it also meant that power could be concentrated in a strongly centralized state. The cult of the divine king, the king on the mountain, was the necessary ideological expression of this new state.

The old kingdoms, loosely held together, with their chieftains, their villages and village communities, were shattered. It was the irrigation system which required that "there shall no longer be more than one king, ruling over all."

Angkor grows up out of pre-Angkorian Cambodia. But it had to transform and change all its traditions, its art, its society. And the consolidation of the central royal authority also meant that the king's freedom of action was circumscribed. He was bound by the requirements of the existing order. His elevation became that of a god. The state was run by an oligarchic aristocracy. The villagers sank to the level of working force, and when mentioned by name in the inscriptions, bear such names as "Dog," "Cat," "Loathsome," "Stinking Brute."

The great canals reached out over the plains, the water of the immense dams glittered in the sunlight, rice paddy upon rice paddy stretching away to the horizon. The new relations of production had released the productive forces, people fell into ever greater misery, and the temples rose ever more vast and beautiful. The surplus grew. The population increased. Labor was in demand and could be exploited.

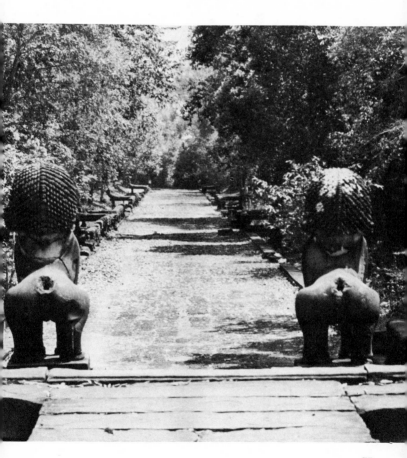

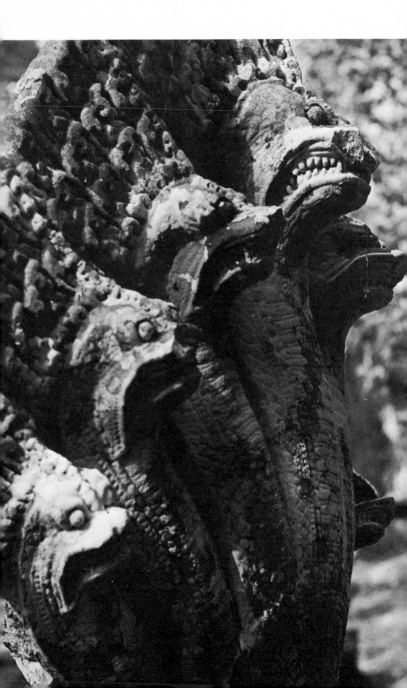

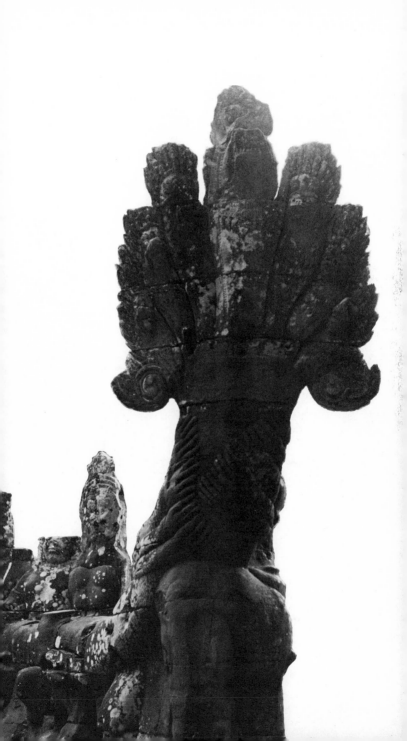

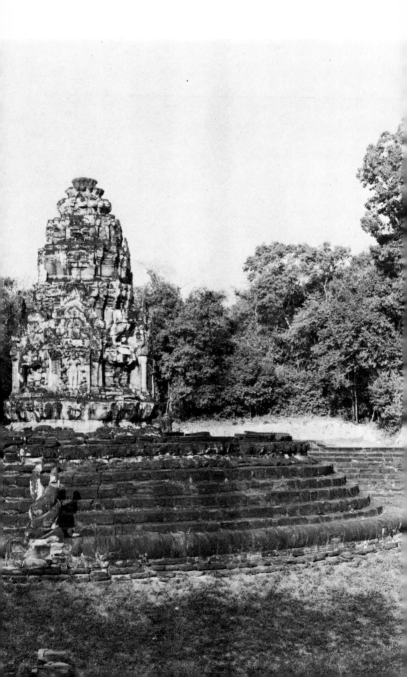

Neak Pean
c. 1180–c. 1190

Jayavarman VII (1181–c. 1218) was a Buddhist. This did not mean the Brahmins had lost their power. It did mean, however, that Neak Pean was created in the Buddhist style.

North of Angkor, Jayavarman VII had had the fourth great irrigation dam constructed. It was smaller than the earlier dams. It only measured 3,827 yards by 984 yards. Neak Pean stood on an island in the middle.

Its architectural form is symbolic. It represents the mythical lake Anavatapta, on the roof of the world, whence flow the four great world rivers.

Neak Pean consists of a basin 76 yards by 76 yards. In the middle of this basin its tower rises from a round platform. At each quarter of the compass outside the central basin lies a smaller basin, measuring 27 yards by 27 yards. In the great basin, apparently on its way in toward the sanctuary, stands the horse Balaha—the shape assumed by the Bodhisattva Lokesvara when he rescued the shipwrecked merchant Simhala and those who were at sea with him, off the coast of Ceylon.

Why the snake?

Outside the gates of the city, the sacred cobra, the naga, raises its seven heads. Coiling itself above their gates, the naga guards each of the temples. Even when the gods change and religions with them, the naga remains. Buddha meditates under its protection. Its hood is his halo.

The Chinese ambassador Chou Ta-kouan—who was of the view that Angkor's architecture was not without a certain harmony—reported that everyone in Angkor told him how every night the king was united with a sacred serpent. This snake, which ruled over all soil in the kingdom, manifested itself nightly in the palace tower in the guise of a woman. Only after the king had lain with her and possessed her could he go to his wives or concubines. If the serpent failed to put in an appearance one night, this foreshadowed the king's death; and if the king himself omitted his duty, disaster would fall.

In legitimizing themselves at Angkor, the kings traced their line back to the ruling families in the earlier kingdoms, and ultimately to the Brahmin Kaundinya who married Soma, the daughter of the naga-king, and founded the dynasty of rulers over the lower Mekong. In order to extend his son-in-law's realm, the naga-king had drunk up all the water and liberated the soil.

There is nothing strange about this snake which watches over the city. The sacred cobra tells us a good deal about the history of Angkor.

The unique thing about Angkor is not that it was a Cambodian kingdom. When Angkor was founded, there had been Cambodian kingdoms with cities and kings, priests, scribes, and merchants for the best part of eight hundred years. In these kingdoms more or less the same language had been spoken as in Angkor, that language that is spoken today. The Angkor kings regarded themselves as descended from the heirs to these kingdoms.

Nor were their religious ideas unique. All the gods of Angkor had existed during earlier centuries. Chinese diplomatic reports from the mid-third century describe gods found later at Angkor and popular customs that still survive

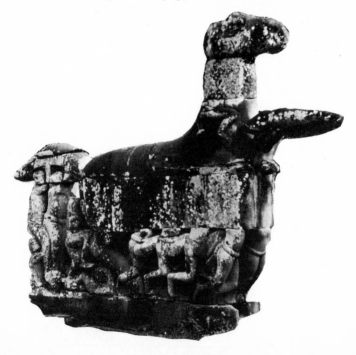

in present-day Cambodia. They also point out that books were being written in an (Indian) script similar to what was in use at that time in Central Asia.

What made Angkor unique was the new irrigation technique, which enabled it to exploit the poor soil north of Tonle Sap and created huge surpluses. But the legend of the naga-king, who had drunk up the water and liberated the soil,

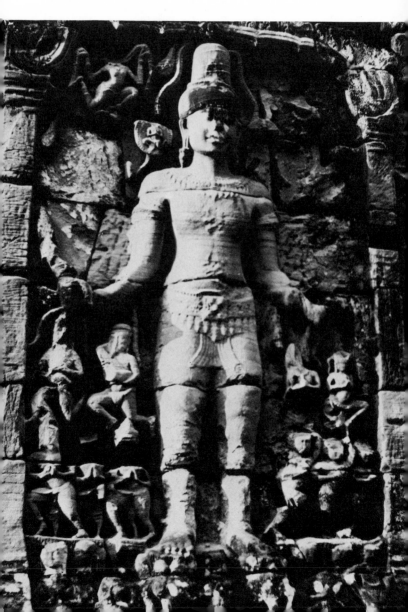

expressed a historical reality. In ancient Fu-nan, the swamps had been utilized. It was this drainage technique which made that culture possible.

The snakes were water spirits, rulers of the Cambodian soil. The fertility rites and symbols, the king's union with the naga or the churning of the Cosmic Ocean—all these were the religious, ideological expressions of the fact that power

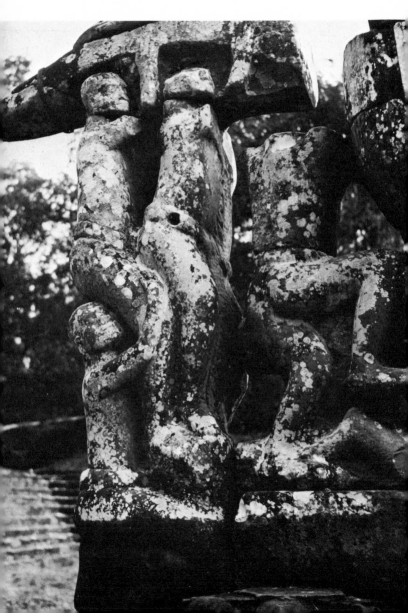

lay in control over the irrigation system. The divinity of the King of Angkor resided in the fact that it was he who took the responsibility to maintain that irrigation system.

But the naga-cult is also interesting on another plane. The Hinduization of the country did not occur by conquest. Nor as a result of any great migration of the peoples (that seductive expression!). What the legend describes is plain, simple

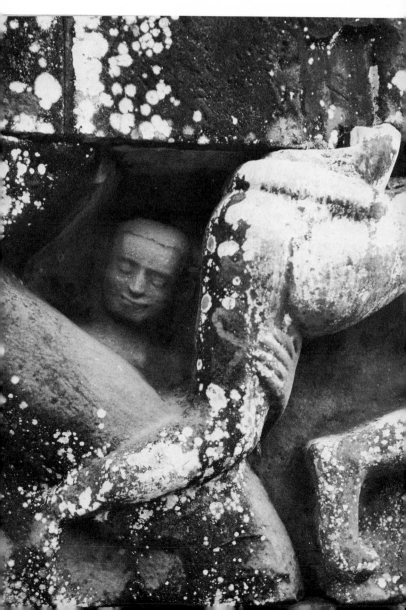

fact. Indian merchants came to Cambodia, as they did to other parts of Southeast Asia. Whether or not they originally were Brahmins is neither here nor there. They became Brahmins, in the same way that Germans and Frenchmen ennobled themselves as soon as they arrived in Sweden, in the seventeenth century.

With them they brought new technical inventions and— very important—an ideology which facilitated the development of a new centralized state. (When the Germanic peoples became Christian, there was no migration of peoples away from the Mediterranean. But one type of society was shattered, and the new type of society adopted the ideological guise best suited to its own needs.)

The Brahmins performed the same function in Cambodia as they did in southern India. They were an intellectually trained cadre, capable of taking over the administration of the new type of state.

It is also striking to see how regularly they married into the reigning families at Angkor. The caste question is without importance; Brahmins and Kshatriyas mingle incessantly and trace their ancestries from nagas. Angkor is dominated by a single intermarried oligarchy.

Into the religious cult the Brahmins assimilated every local legend, The priestly function, one might say, was to find the right political solution to ideological conflicts. And under the general super-ideology—according to which the kingship was derived from the gods—they found room for all sorts of contradictory elements.

When Buddha—who is also the king—meditates under the protective hood of the naga-king, this is an image based on sacred texts. But long before Buddha, the naga was sacred all over India and Southeast Asia. And the sacredness of the texts is open to question. In the course of their political struggle to regain a material power which in India had been shaken by Buddhism, the Brahmins wrote suitable texts concerning the naga and Buddha. The motif is most frequently exploited in Khmer art, where it came in handy in view of the political need to fuse popular superstition and legitimacy with oligarchy and royalty.

The serpent is not fortuitous. Nor is it to be understood in terms of texts and religious meditations. It is historical, it is social.

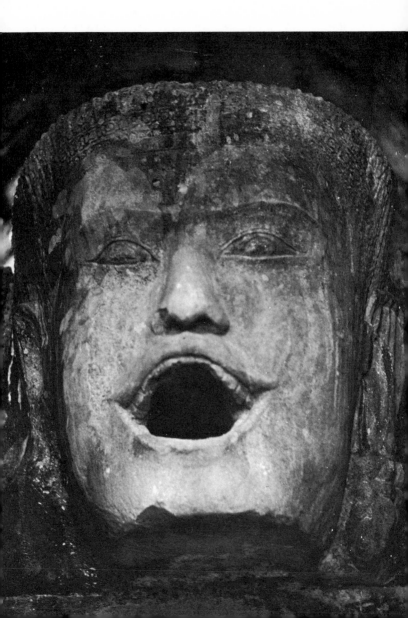

Ta Prohm
1186

Jayavarman VII was a great builder. He improved the road system, and along the major highways caused inns to be erected every seven to nine miles. According to his own inscription, he erected 121 inns.

He also built 102 regional hospitals, as well as a number of hospitals in cities. These had doctors, nurses, and other personnel. The hospitals owned 838 villages with 81,640 working inhabitants, who delivered 11,192 tons of rice to the hospital administration every year. Further, the hospitals annually received, among much else, 4,683 pounds of sesame, 232 pounds of cinnamon, 3,402 muscatel nuts, 48,000 potions against fever, and 1,960 boxes of hemorrhoid ointment.

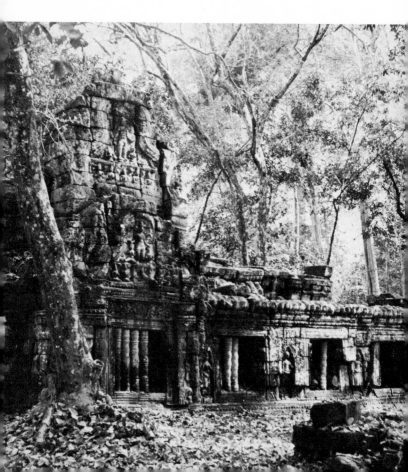

But his religious building works were even more extensive. Ta Prohm was erected to house the image of Jayavarman VII's mother. Within the temple area, 16,640 persons had their dwellings. In the temple itself, 18 of the higher priesthood, 2,740 petty clergy, and 2,232 servants—among them 615 temple dancers—were employed. Five years later, Jayavarman VII had Preah Khan erected in memory of his father, Dharanindravarman II, where the latter was worshipped in the shape of the Bodhisattva Lokesvara (employing, among others, 1,000 temple dancers).

These were large buildings, hastily built. Good sandstone was now rare. Thousands upon thousands of workers toiled on the building of these temples, and monumentality took the place of craftsmanship.

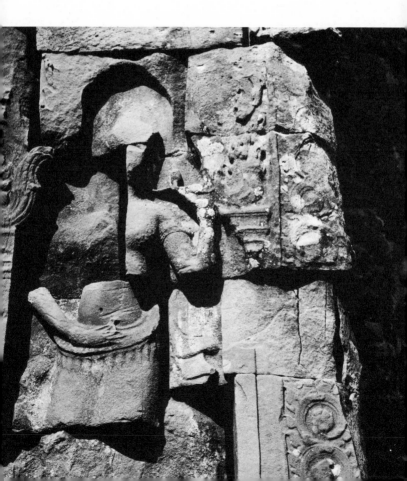

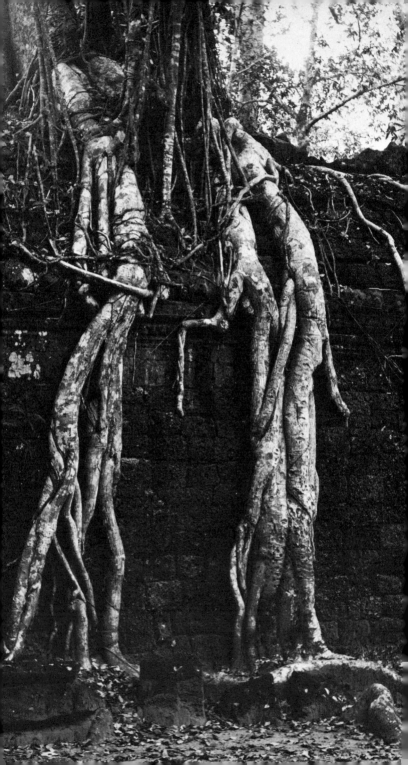

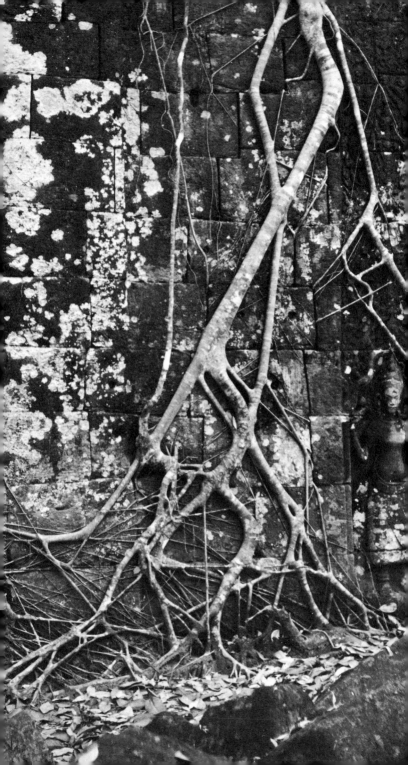

These temples were not open to the public. There was no public. They were not, could not be, cathedrals in the medieval European sense. Later, Angkor Vat became just that—but only after Angkor had fallen and the Khmer Kingdom had been crushed and new economic relationships between people had come into being, and the religion had changed. The temples served the gods and the kings, who had been elevated to the rank of gods, and the higher officials, whose status was also divine. Outsiders got no further than the galleries (which were also used for storing grain).

Since the temples were not places of popular assembly, it may seem as if they served no social purpose and that their numbers were without rhyme or reason. It could be said—and many have said—that the Khmer Kingdom "built itself to death."

Yet these temples had a perfectly concrete social function. The revolution in agricultural techniques in the ninth century had made it possible to exploit soil which until then had only been of marginal use. Where previously the soil had been fertilized by burning-over, it was now possible to carry on intensive irrigational agriculture. But to carry through this transformation a social and political revolution had been needed. The new irrigation technique meant an intensive exploitation of labor. It called for long-term economic planning and great investments. It made necessary a centralized bureaucracy. The Brahmins and the temples gave it an organizational framework. Just as the petty kings and independent provincial lords had to be crushed before the new irrigation technique could be exploited, so the power of the temple bureaucracy grew. They regulated the irrigation system. They ruled over the soil and the villages.

To build a temple was to cultivate soil. The temples thus were necessary. The peasants were working for the gods. The temples distributed the surplus. By the time the system was fully extended, the temple of Ta Prohm had 3,140 villages, and 79,365 individuals were working for it. Preah Khan had 5,324 villages, and 97,840 individuals labored in its service.

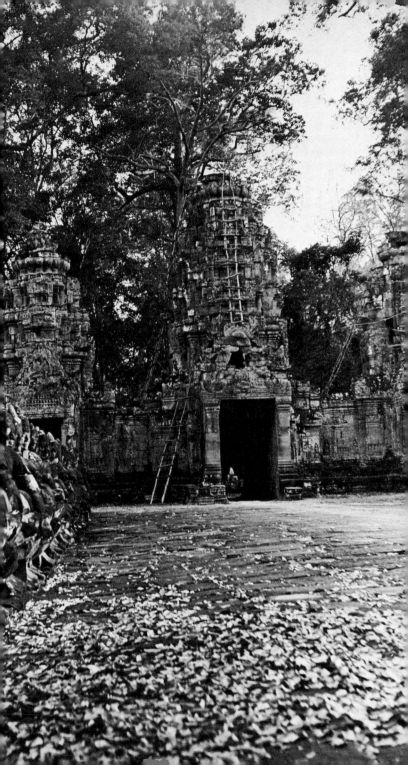

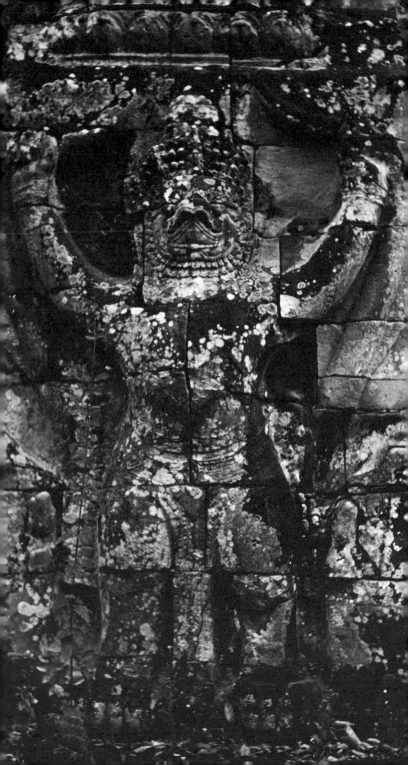

According to one inscription, from the year 1191, 20,000 divinities in gold, silver, bronze, and stone were to be found spread out over the various provinces. They were served by 13,500 villages and 306,372 persons. To these gods 38,000 tons of rice were delivered every year.

This was the temples' economic justification. The divinities and the cult were the form taken by the economic exploitation. The great economic progress made during the ninth century had increased the numbers of the population, increased the yield, made the ruling class ever wealthier and more powerful, and the common people ever poorer.

Religion paid off.

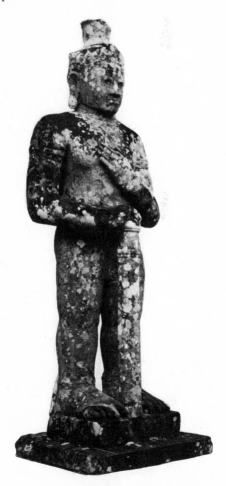

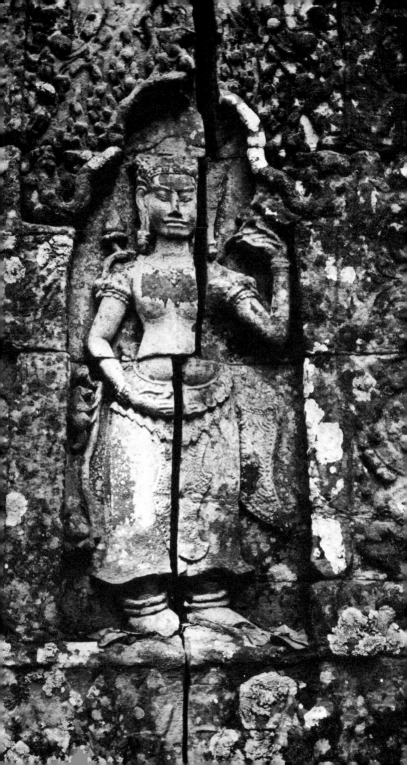

Ta Som
c. 1190

Srah Sang
c. 1190

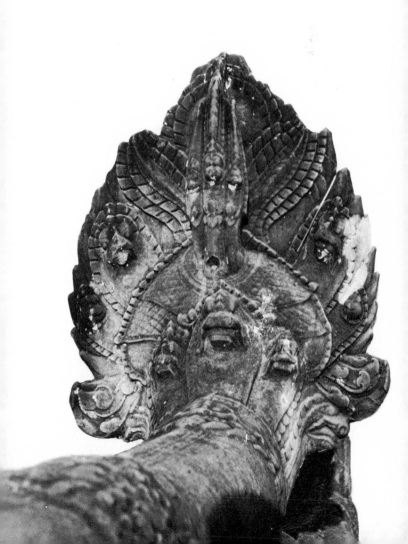

Bayon
c. 1190–c. 1218

Bayon was the central temple in the city raised by Jayavarman VII. It was also the temple in which the cult of the divinity and the cult of the king found their most forceful expression. From all its towers, the face of Lokesvara, the All-Seeing, the Merciful, stares out over the city and the kingdom. The Bodhisattva looks toward all four quarters of the compass. But he is also the king. The monumental faces become portraits. It is power, looking out over its kingdom. ("Before my face . . . Let the light of thy countenance shine upon us . . .")

But it wasn't only the King Lokesvara who was worshipped there. At Bayon had been assembled all the provincial cults of the realm and all cults of the royal ancestors. This temple was the most sublime—and most baroque—expression of the grandeur of power. Yet it was itself carelessly built, often altered during its construction, and never completed. We are conscious of a profound inner contradiction, of grandeur based on sub-solid foundations. This makes Bayon not merely an expression of the sublimity of power, but also of its inherent contradictions, its inevitable decay.

Of all the temples, furthermore, Bayon is the one which has most fascinated visitors and tourists. It has nothing of Angkor Vat's "classical" lines. It is baroque. In all nineteenth-century accounts, its stone faces stare out at us from a tangle of lianas and vegetation—great silent faces capable of satisfying any reasonable demands on "Asiatic mysticism." The architectural idea underlying Bayon also corresponds closely to the one underlying our own cities. Instead of its stone faces we have neon signs—but Bayon, too, is a "city center." Nor are these similarities fortuitous. Bayon was the last of the great buildings and expressed the last huge expansion of power. An expansion which contained within itself the certainty of its own imminent dissolution.

I have used datings. I have delineated the various historical periods. Jayavarman VII has appeared in these pages as a great ruler. But now I must point out that all these datings are themselves of recent date. In 1927, Philippe Stern, on the basis of the French archaeologists' work, could sit in Paris and

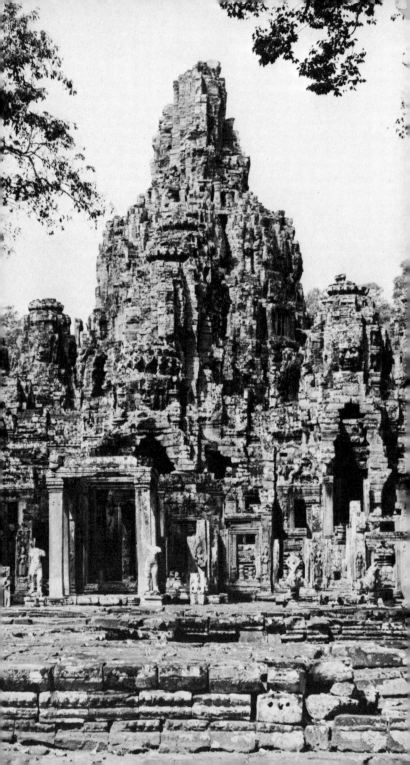

figure out an entirely new chronology for Angkor. Not until he had done so was it possible for field workers to prove him right. Only then could they define the issues and clarify the historical sequence of events.

French imperialism was just as cruel, just as inhuman, as the British, or the German, or the United States'. (Anyone who is curious to read of the part played by the French in old Indochina can turn to the early writings of Ho Chi Minh.) Nevertheless, there were certain specific traits. At Angkor the French scientists did great work. They even managed to check such plunder as the British administrators in India not only winked at but themselves engaged in.

Concerning Angkor, James Fergusson, the great Scottish architectural historian, wrote in his *History of Indian and Eastern Architecture:*

> Few things are more humiliating to an Englishman than to compare the intelligent interest and liberality the French display in these researches, contrasted with the stolid indifference and parsimony of the English in like matters.

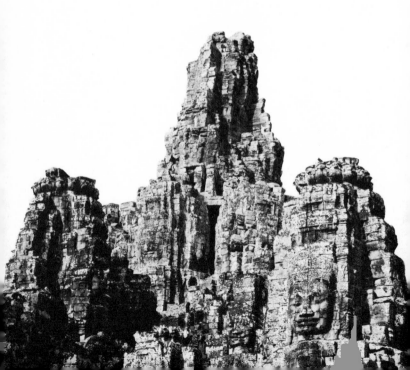

Two hundred yards east of the Konarak Temple at Orissa, in India, lies a huge stone block. It has been hacked at. Once it had its place over the eastern entrance of the temple. Its reliefs were irreplaceable. In 1893, the British, intending to drag it to Calcutta, pried it loose. But the effort proved too great. Once Indians had transported it 300 miles, from the quarries to Konarak, and there lifted it into position. As late as the 1950s, British-trained Indian civil servants were still turning a blind eye to the plunder of "unprotected monuments" by Western diplomats stationed in Delhi and their accomplices. The French archaeologists had had Malraux jailed for less. Even as early as the 1890s, they had ensured that Angkor was scheduled as a protected monument.

I do not write this to eulogize French imperialism. But there was, admittedly, a certain difference. Though there is no "exculpating" imperialism just because it did some restoration work at Angkor. (This would have been carried out even without the French, if Cambodia had been left in peace. After all, as late as 1577 the Cambodians had done their own restoration work.) Still, we mustn't forget that the French did imprison Malraux for his thievery.

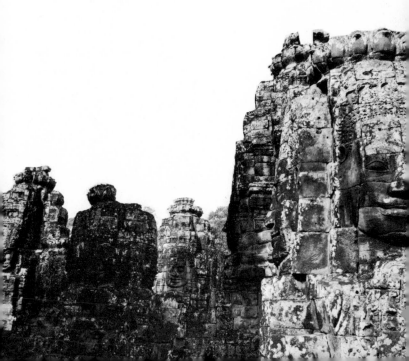

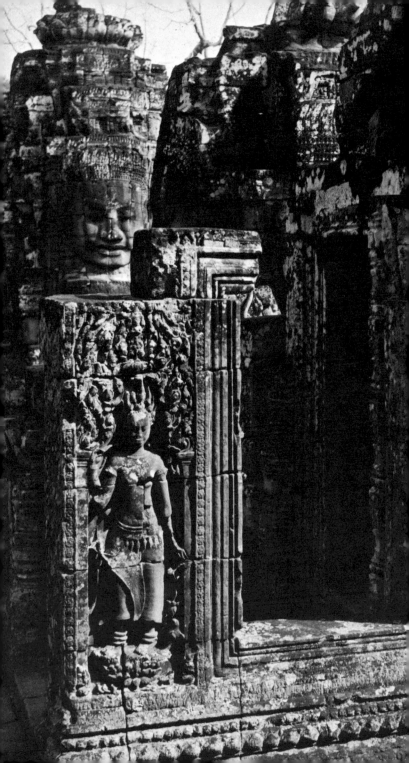

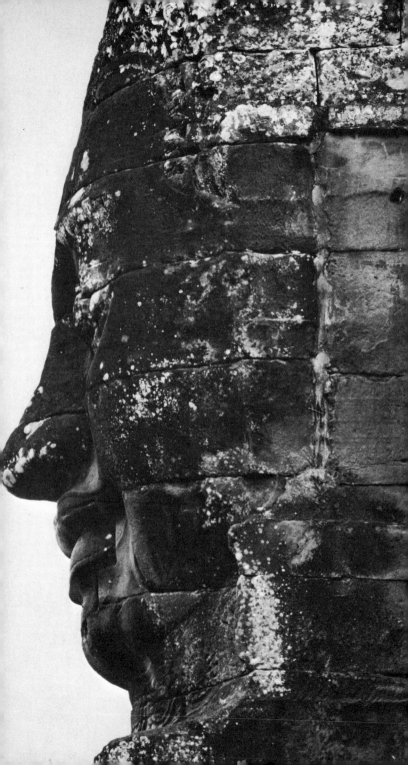

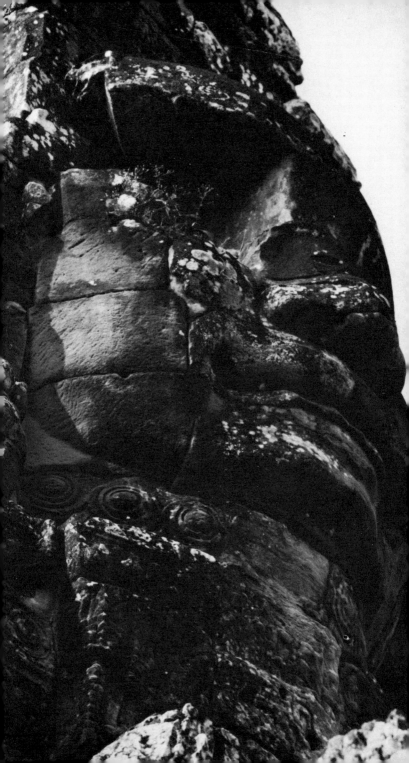

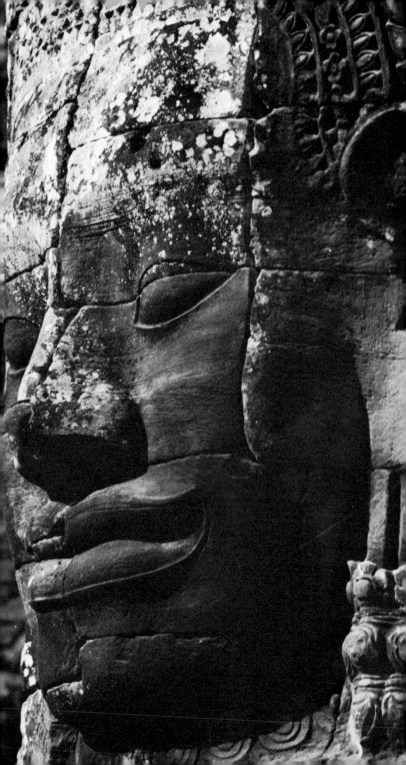

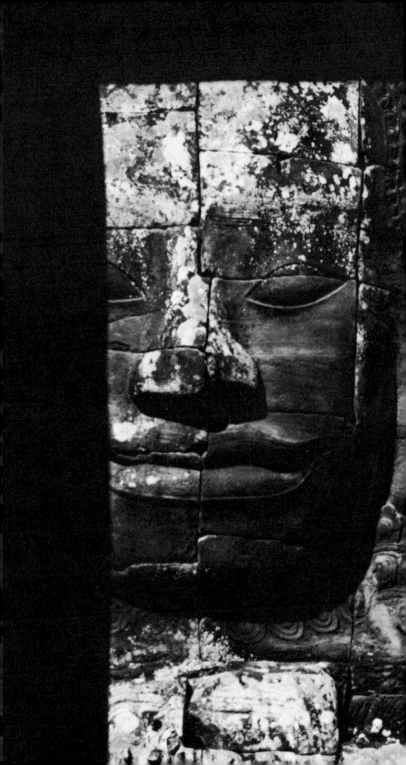

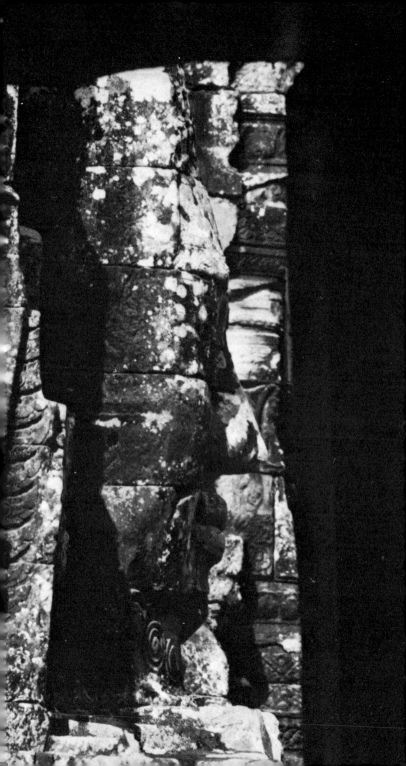

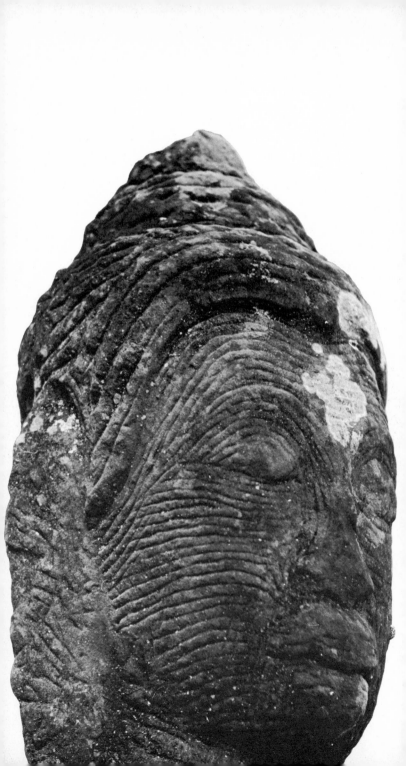

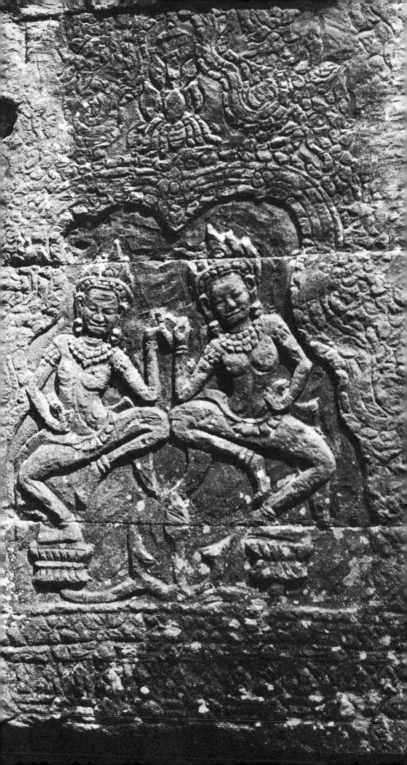

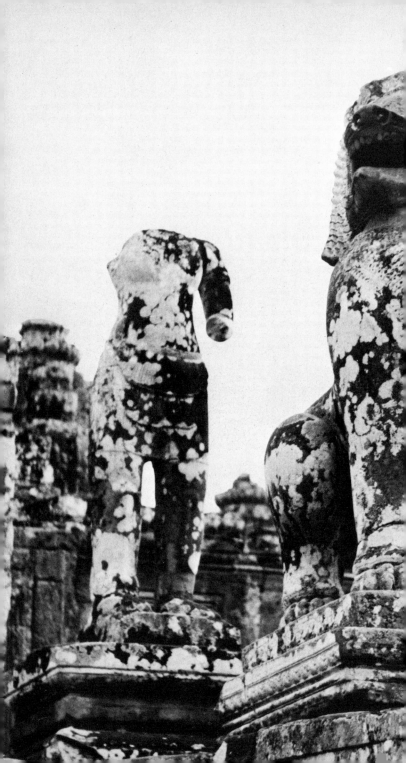

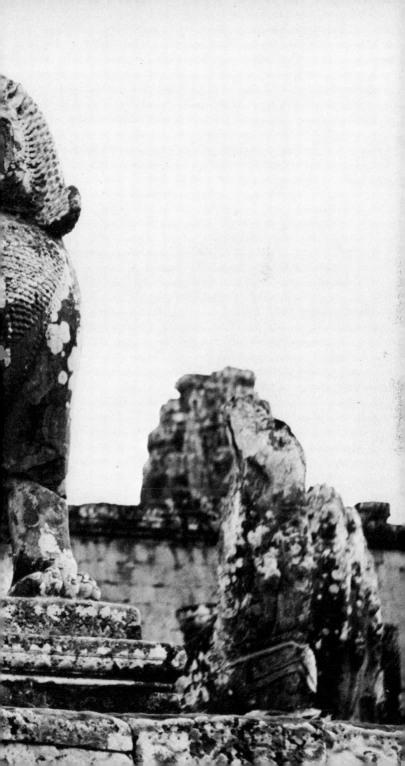

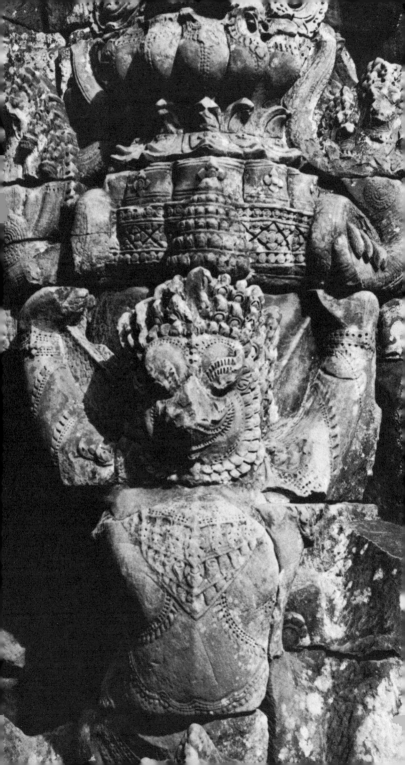

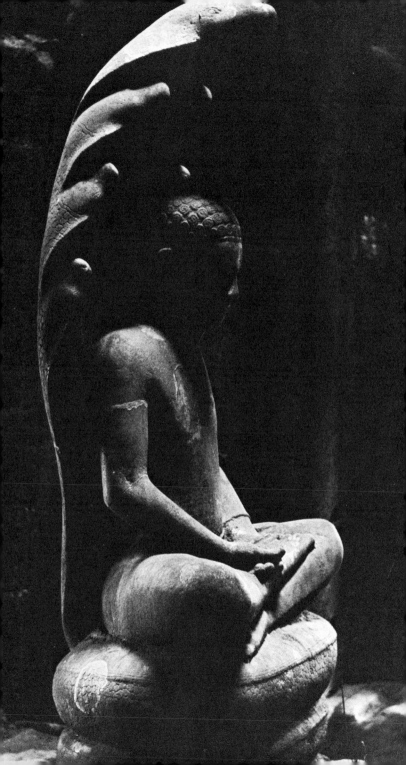

Bayon, bas-reliefs, the outer gallery
c. 1190–c. 1218

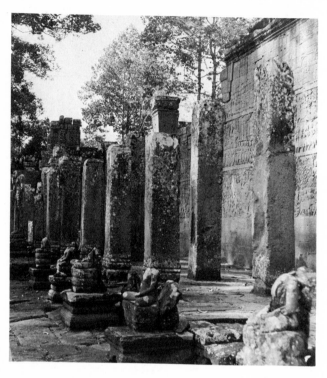

The temple is surrounded by two galleries. The outer forms
a rectangle measuring 153 yards by 175 yards, and the inner
a rectangle measuring 76 yards by 87 yards. The inner walls
of the galleries are 13 feet high, of which 11.5 feet are covered
with bas-reliefs. On the northern side these reliefs remain
unfinished. It is supposed that on the death of Jayavarman
VII the artists simply stopped work.

The reliefs in the inner gallery have mythological motifs.
In the outer gallery—to which the "common people" had
access—they are the "battle paintings," and bear the hall-
mark of an everyday realism. A patriotic (historical solecism!)
history lesson in stone; their realism is down-to-earth (dog-
fights, cooking, agriculture, etc.) and not dissimilar in character to our own Scandinavian churches' medieval murals.

These reliefs were intended to be "read." Walking round the temple, keeping the murals all the time on one's right-hand side, one "reads" them from right to left, not, as we read our alphabet, from left to right.

The reliefs are divided in distinct planes. A man, killed in battle, sinks to the bottom of the lake—not into "the underworld." Beneath him other events are being played out on the lake shore. A simple and unambiguous solution to the "legibility" problem! If art historians have worried their heads over questions of perspective, this mostly goes to show they simply haven't understood the nature of these artists' task: to sculpt legible narrative reliefs.

The battle-scene narratives are historical. In 1177 a fleet from Champa had entered Tonle Sap. Smashing all Khmer resistance, taking Angkor, it had slain the usurper then enthroned there. But Jayavarman continued the war against the Champa forces, and after several battles, won a naval engagement which seems to have proved decisive. In 1181 he was able to take Angkor and crown himself king. His subsequent foreign policy was described in the mid-thirteenth century by the inspector of foreign trade at Fukien, Chau Ju-kua, as follows:

> From of old this country (Cambodia) had maintained close neighborly relations with Champa, and sent it yearly a tribute of gold; but on the fifteenth of the fifth moon of the fourth year of the *shun-hi* period (of the Sung, i.e., 1177) the ruler of Champa surprised the capital (of Cambodia) with his fleet, and on the refusal of their demands for peace (the people) were slaughtered. From that time the bitterest enmity and a thirst for revenge existed (in Cambodia). In the fifty-sixth year of the cycle in the *k'ing-yüan* period (i.e., 1199) (Cambodia) invaded Champa with a powerful army, made the sovereign prisoner, put to death his ministers, and nearly exterminated the people, after which it made a man of Cambodia sovereign of Champa, and down to the present day it has remained a dependency of Cambodia.

As for the good neighborly relations prevailing before 1177, we should perhaps—as we have seen before—take them with a pinch of salt. But the stone relief's dying men on this wall are not "art." They are pictures of folk who have just been put to death.

The bas-reliefs at Bayon are regarded as less artistic than those at Angkor Vat. This is open to question. Personally I find their directness and their realism highly artistic. It is art from the age of Khmer greatness and collapse.

For Bayon was its last great building work. The greatness of Angkor and Jayavarman VII's all-seeing face were expressive of the inevitability of that collapse. Jayavarman VII set his builders to work. He himself did not build. The builders, the sculptors, were craftsmen. It was the "stinking beasts" who set their stamp on the all-seeing monarch's work. Theirs was a realistic art. In an age of sharpening class warfare even art that lauds the establishment expresses its imminent collapse.

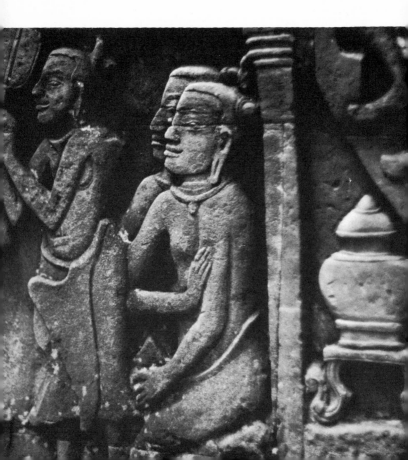

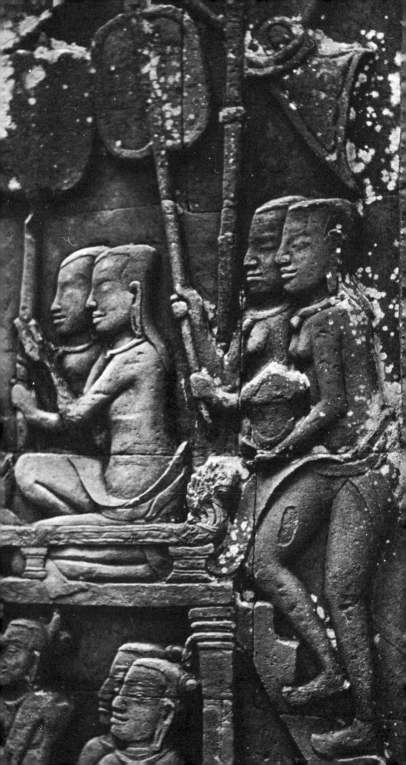

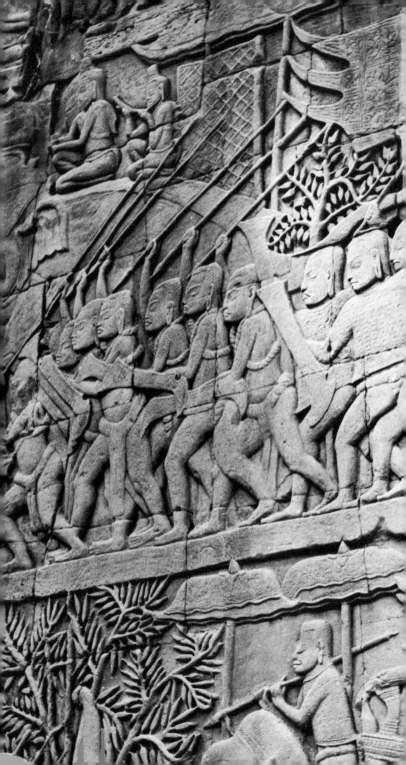

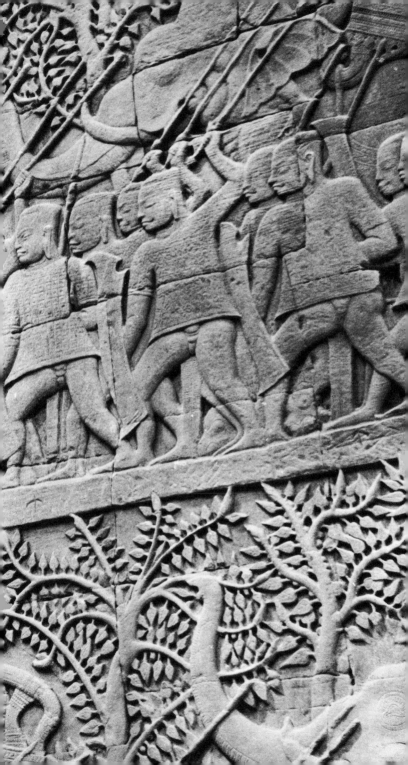

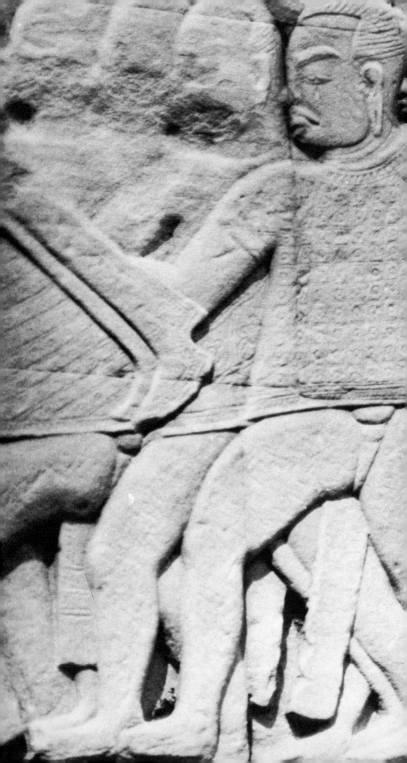

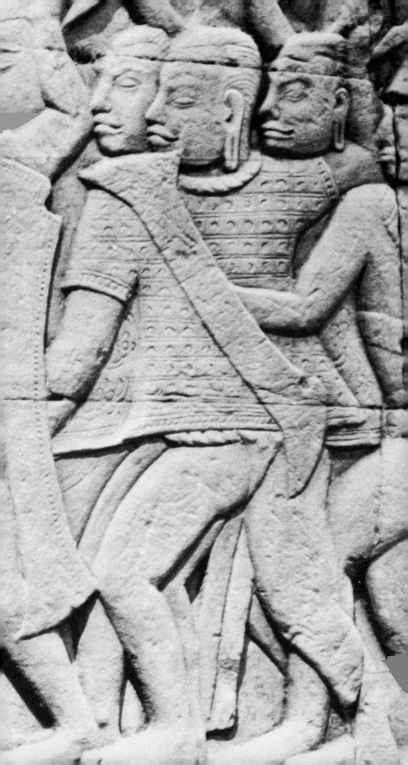

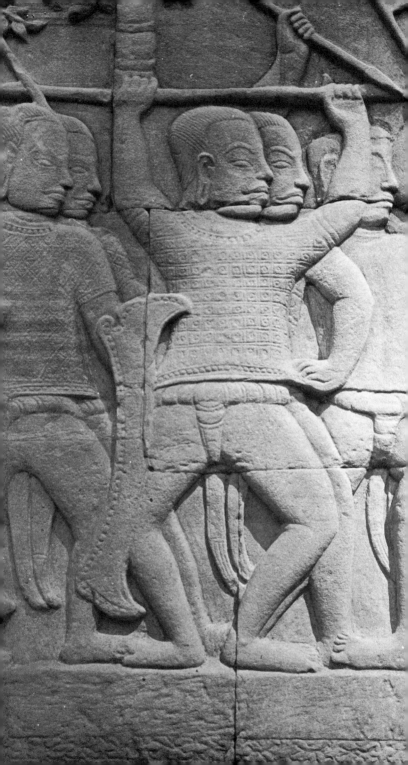

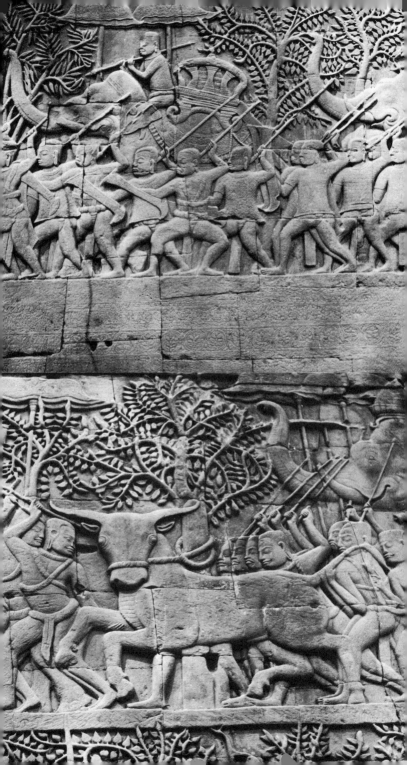

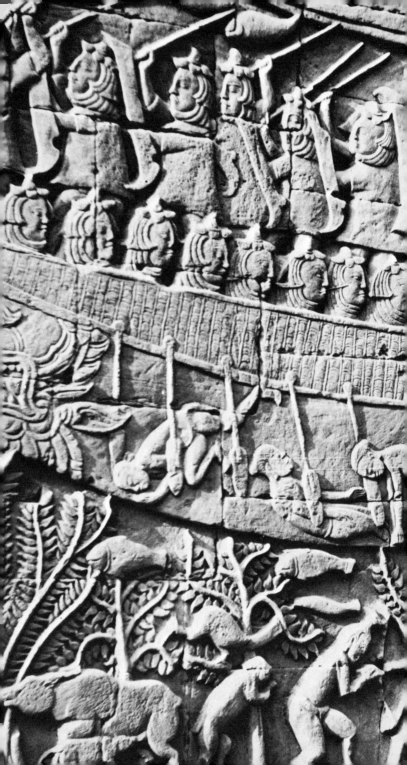

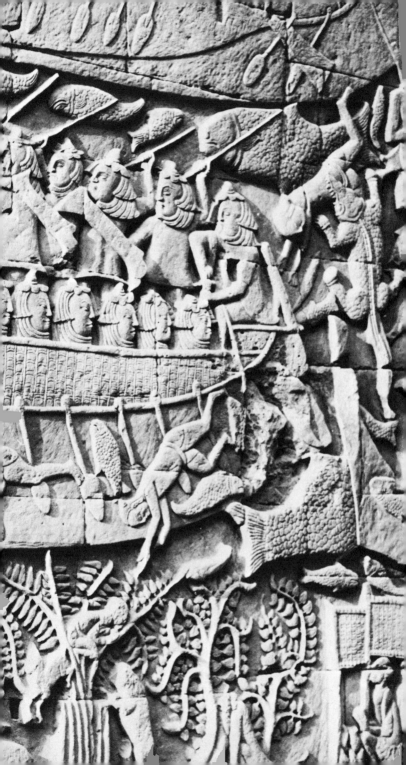

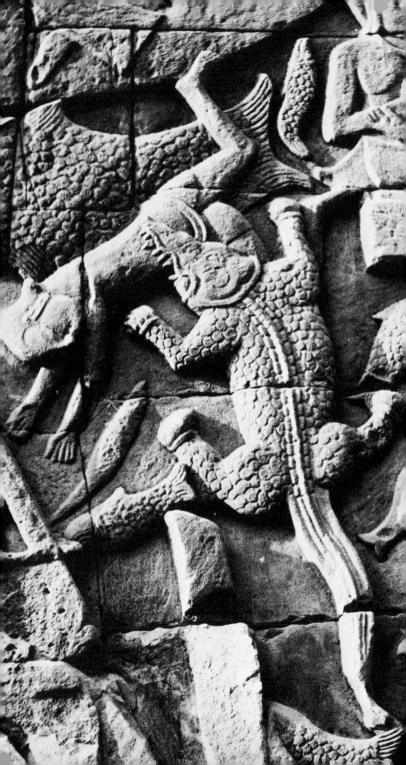

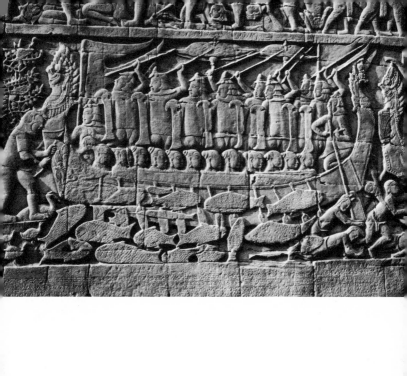
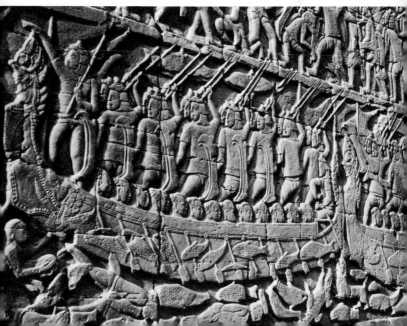

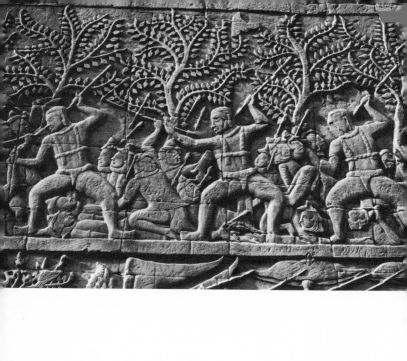

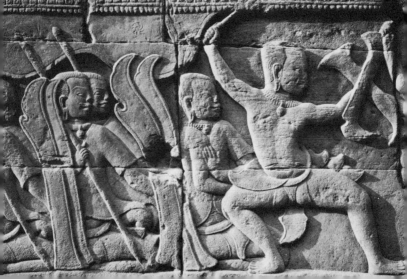

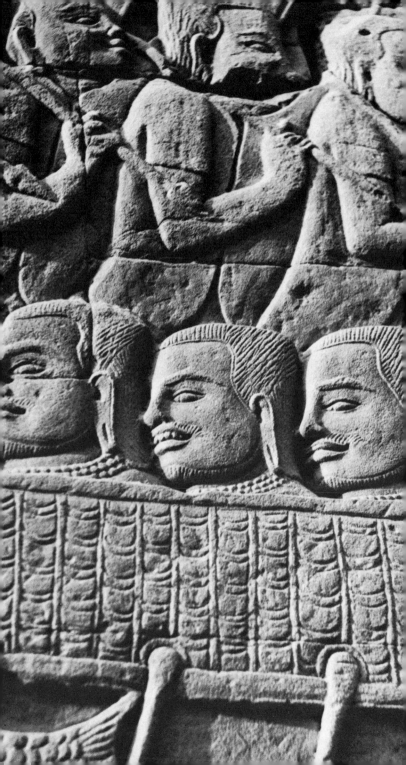

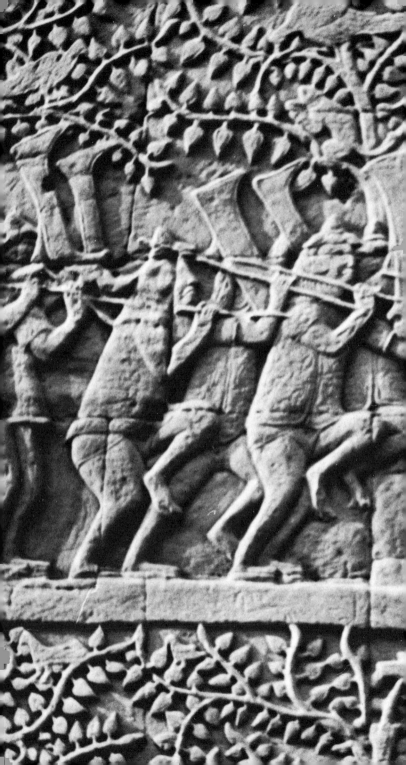

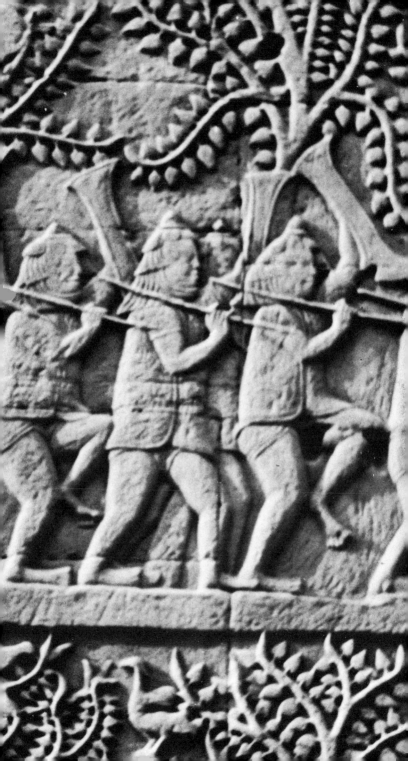

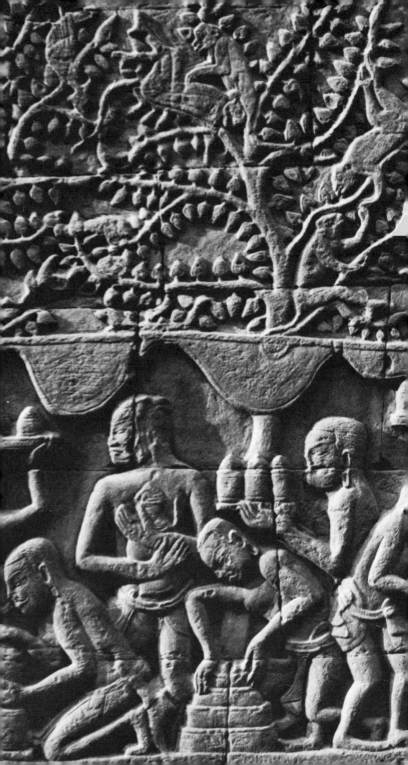

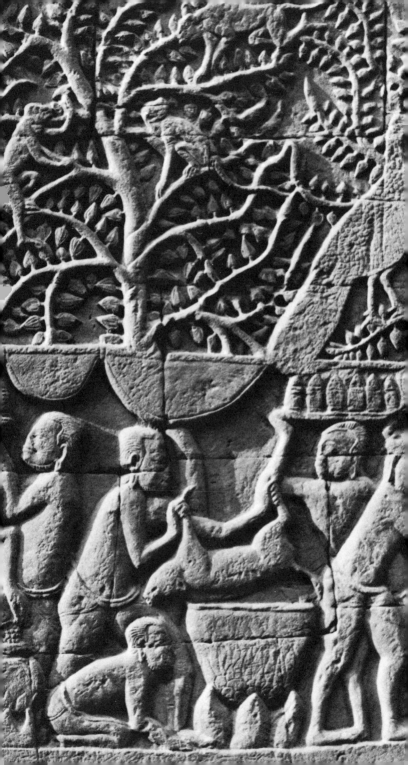

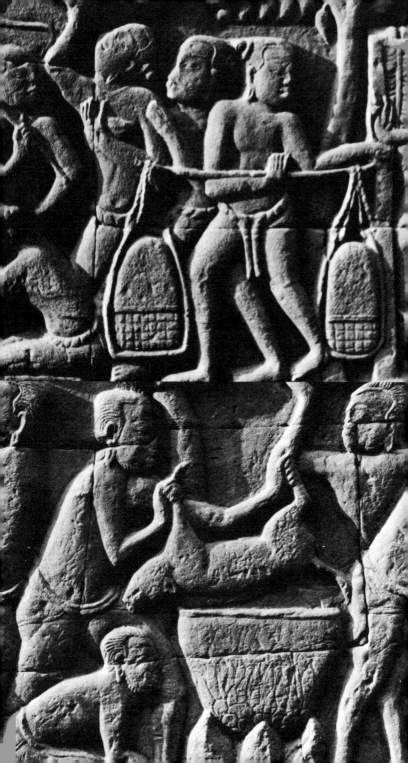

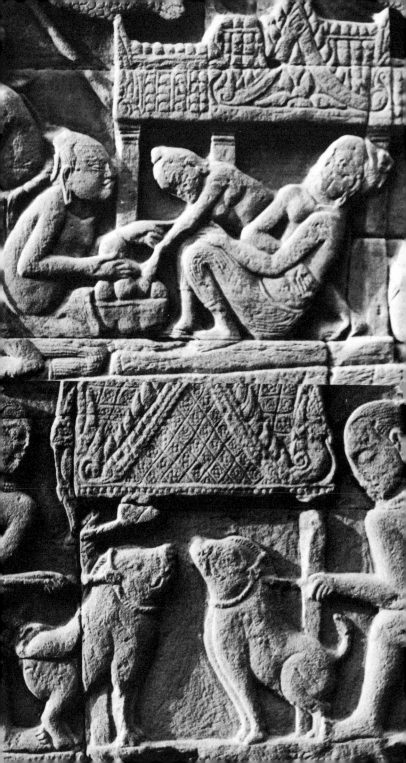

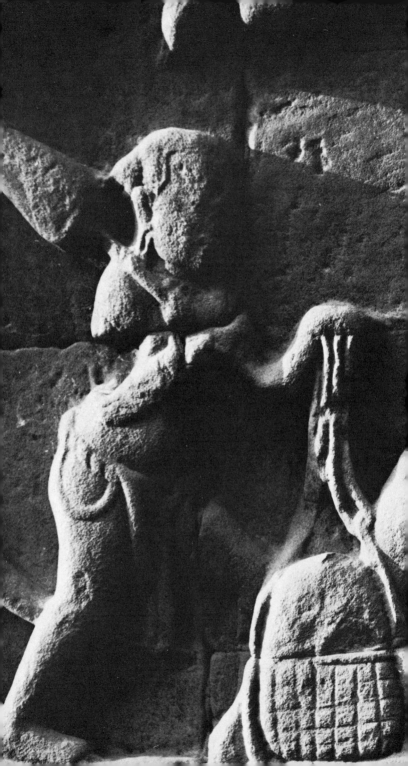

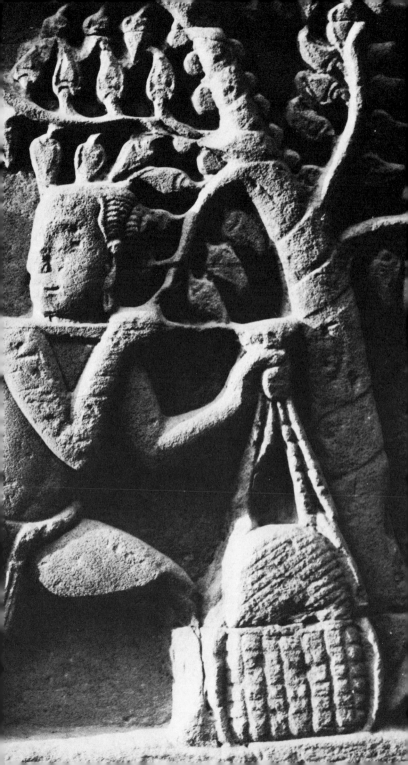

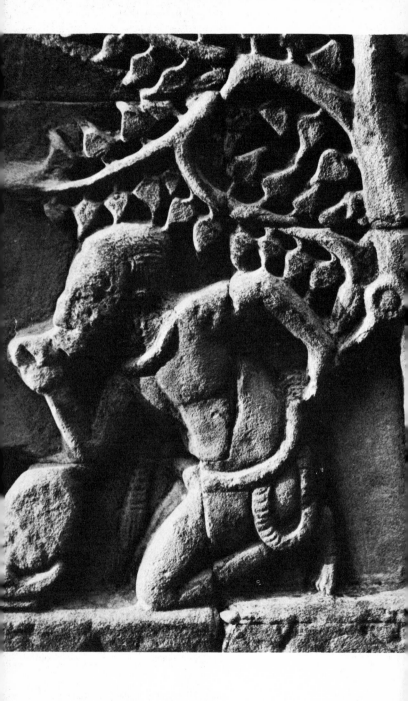

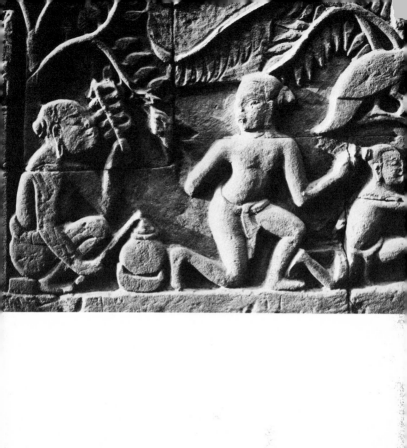

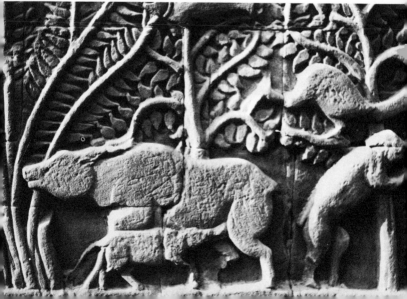

The reliefs are unfinished. And this makes it possible for us to see exactly how these craftsmen, these slaves, these artists, worked. How the figures, first drawn out, were then cut out. But the unfinished reliefs tell us something else, too.

Gun had been photographing them, feeling them with her fingers. She said:

"The craftsmen were at work here while the old masters sat in the shade, talking. Now and then they came over, to keep an eye on the work. Then one of the apprentices comes running. He shouts: 'Now he's dead!' At this the craftsmen stopped hacking at the stone wall and put down their tools. But the old masters rushed over and said: 'Calm down now! We've heard that again and again! If you don't get on with your work you'll be in trouble.' The craftsmen ignored their masters' words. All they said was: 'Well—at last he's dead!' And went off home. After a while the masters, too, went home, muttering to themselves: 'We'll be in trouble, you'll see, we'll get into trouble.'"

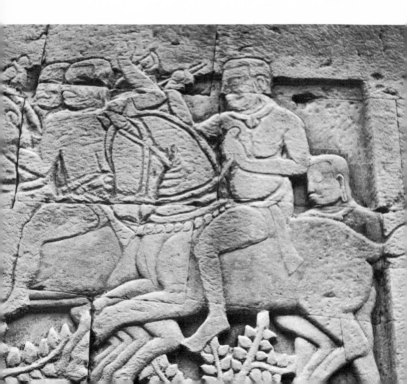

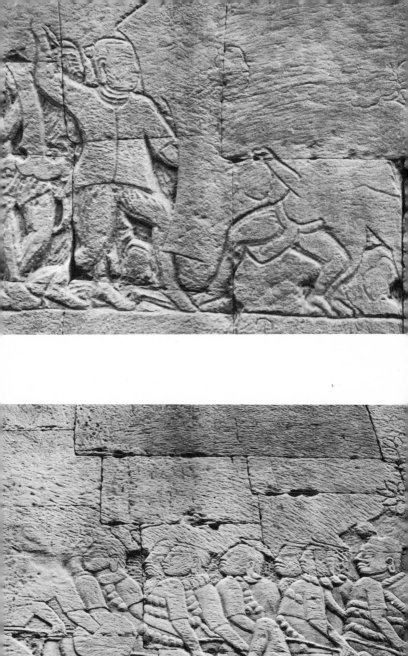

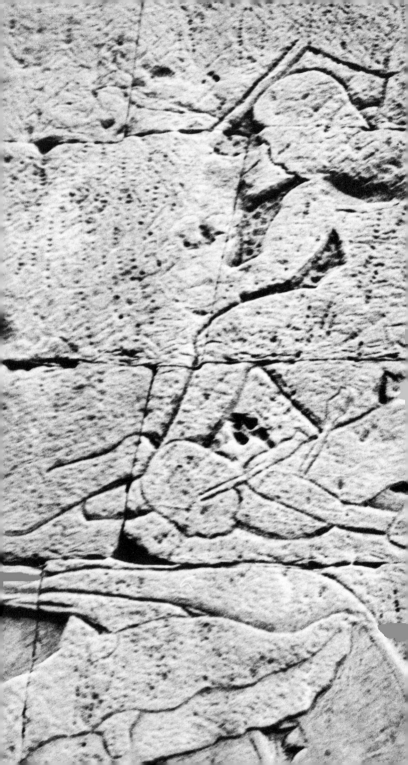

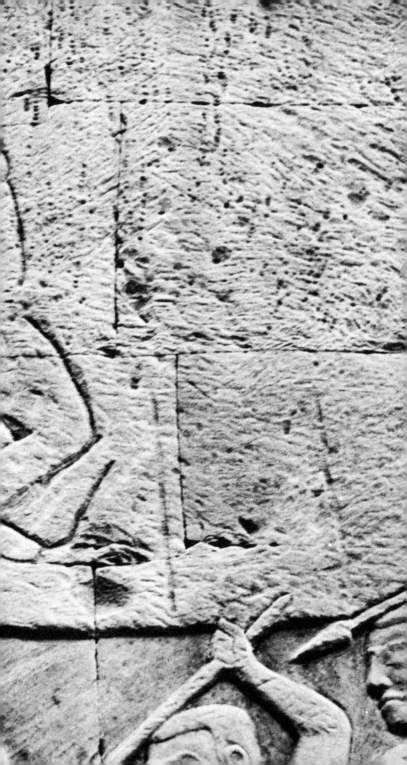

Angkor Thom. The Terraces
c. 1190–1218

The new city which Jayavarman VII had built, with Bayon as its city center, occupied more or less the same area as the city which had been captured by the Champa troops in 1177. The whole town was a sanctuary, one great shrine, not unlike the Kremlin. The city gates were the outer gates of the temple. Closed at night, they were open in the daytime. No dogs were admitted. Or criminals (known by their cropped ears). The whole city was symbolic. Outside its gates, gods and demons tugged at the naga, and in the central temple the Ocean of the Cosmos was churned up like butter by the god-king. He was the power. And the glory. An extremely concrete piece of symbolism. It wasn't the Cosmic Ocean he churned up—it was the common people.

The rebuilding of the city had meant the restoration of the irrigation system, its development and its centralization. For the last time the administrative machine was restored. But in religious matters there had already been a change—the king's magnificence, his face, which shone down over the kingdom, was eloquent of the cramp which was holding society in its grasp.

After Jayavarman VII came a religious reaction. Then a

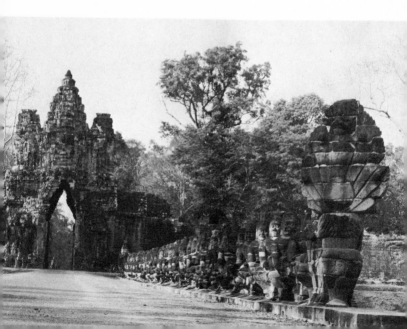

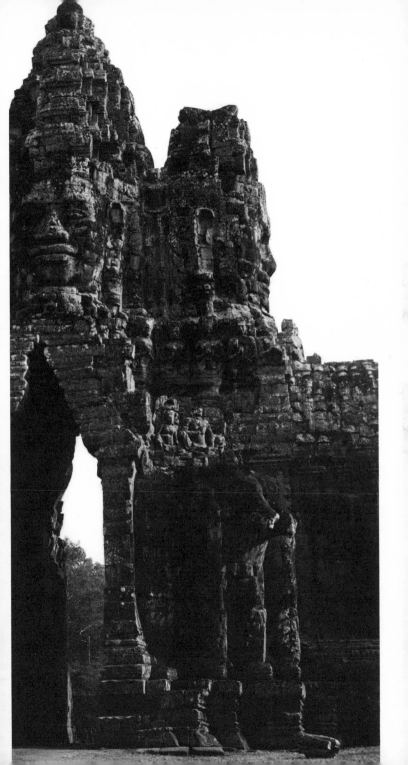

further change of religion. J. K. Fairbank, the great authority, put it like this:

> Soon after this effort the great age of Khmer architecture came to an end. The spread of the simple and austere Theravada form of Buddhism from Ceylon among the Khmer people seems to have undermined the prestige and power of the god-king as an incarnate Siva or Buddha.

But was it really so? Did "new thoughts" or "agitators" appear out of somewhere and change people's ideas of reality and so change their society?

Or—differently expressed: Could Angkor have survived if only the "agitators" and "dangerous thoughts" had been excluded from the realm?

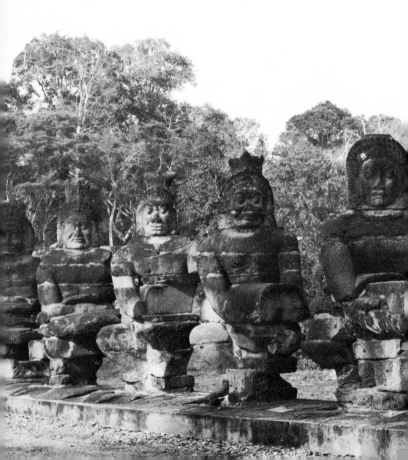

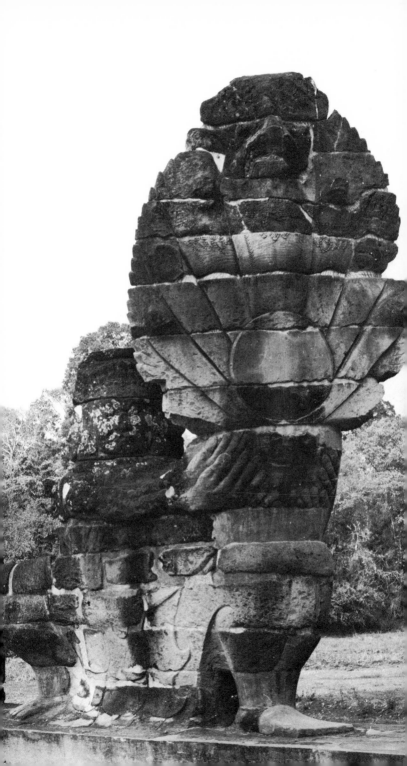

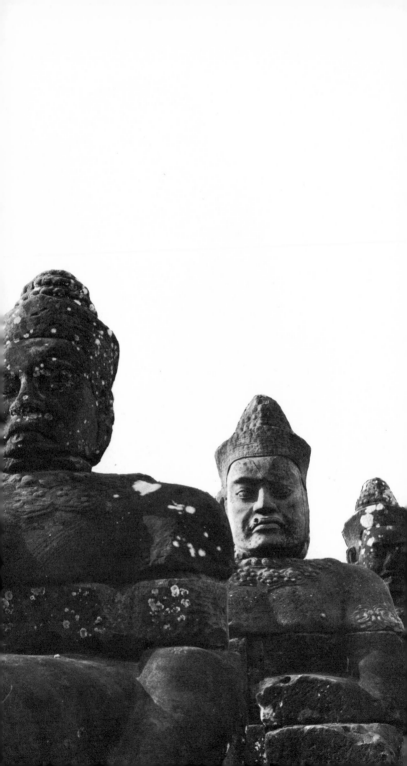

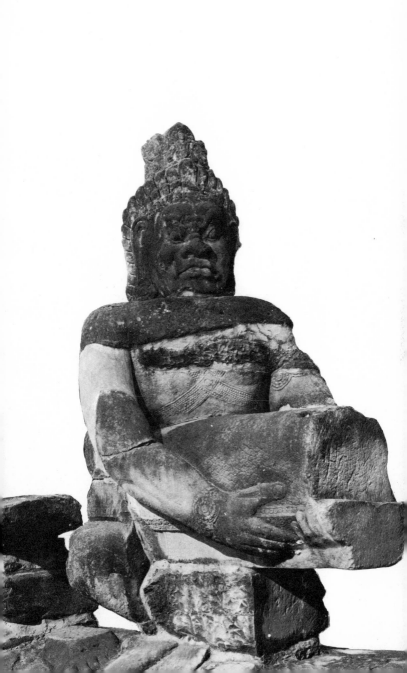

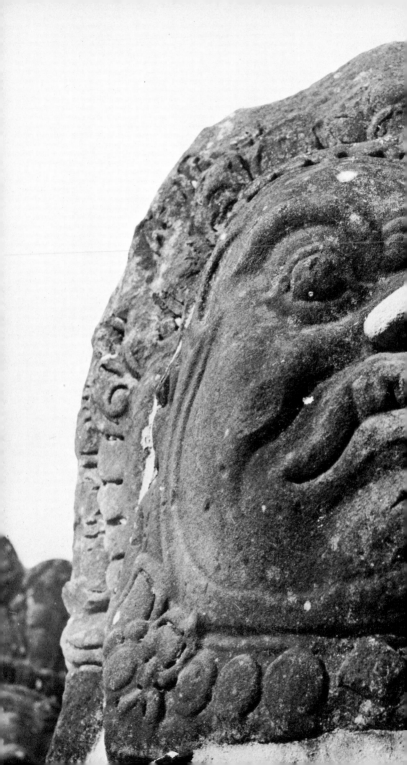

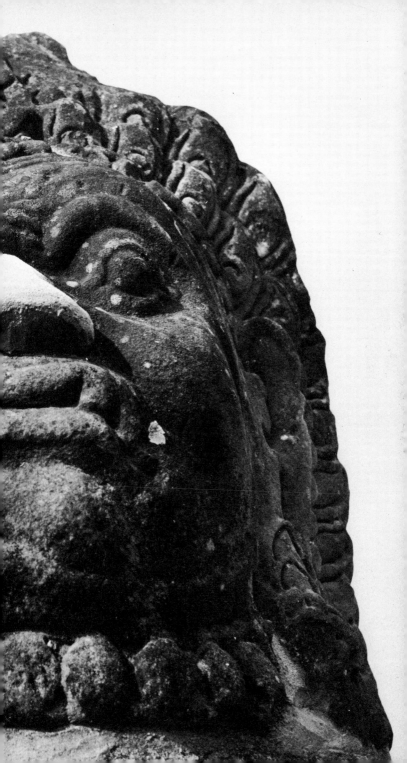

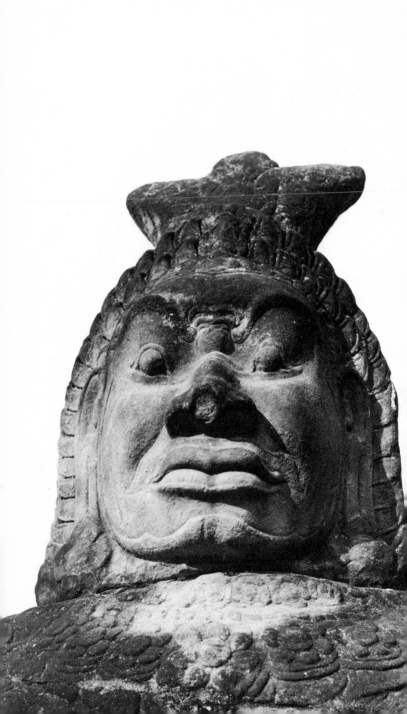

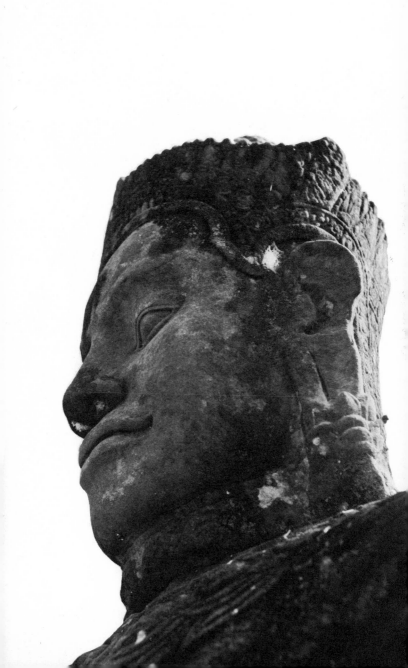

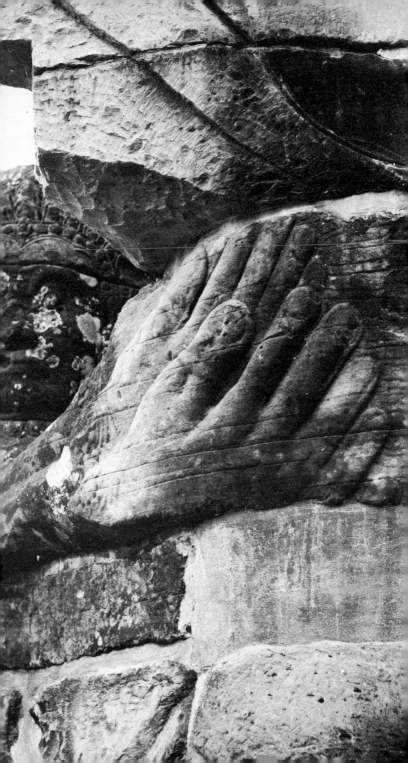

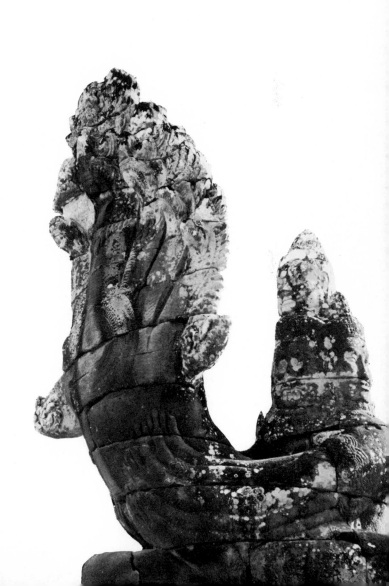

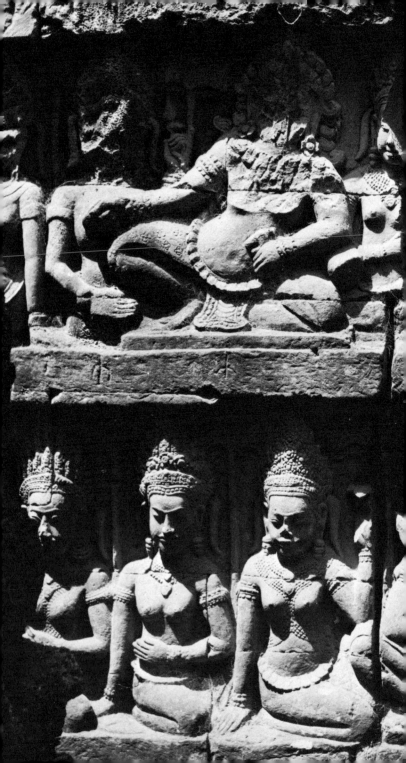

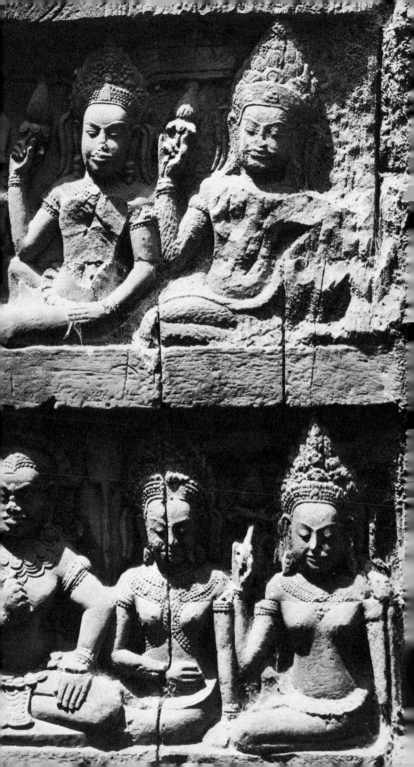

From the sweat of other people's brows

"Recently, during the war with Siam, the (villages) have been totally wiped out," reports Chou Ta-kouan from his embassy at Angkor in 1296–1297. The hundred years war against Champa had been extended. A new war, which was to last for several centuries, had begun. Once again, Jayavarman VII's successor tried to get the irrigation system to work. But the new wars ravaged the realm.

In 1349, it is true, Wang Ta-yuan could still describe the wealth to be seen in the market outside the south gate of the city of Angkor and speak of "rich and great Cambodia," but our information about the kings of Angkor becomes steadily sparser, its history ever more obscure (the archives, don't forget, have been burned). Finally, in 1431, Angkor is abandoned. The city is no longer defensible. Gradually the capital is removed to Phnom Penh.

One could explain Angkor's fall—and some writers have— as an outcome of all the wars. Again and again its rulers tried to establish an empire; again and again they sought to expand. And again and again new wars ravaged the country. In the end, Cambodia, rich and powerful Cambodia, bled to death.

But this is an inadequate explanation. One can no more attribute Angkor's decline to the wars than to a change of religion. Wars were fought. And the religion changed. But it is not here we have to seek the cause of Angkor's decline. Nor does it suffice to say the rulers of Angkor "overbuilt themselves."

Angkor perished. But Cambodia survived. The rulers vanished. But not the people. The whole history of Angkor was a history of incessant revolts, of unending social struggle. What happened between the thirteenth and the fifteenth centuries was something much greater than a change of religion. Something that went much deeper than mere warfare.

Angkor grew up as a centralized state, in which, by exploiting new techniques, oligarchy had been able, at the people's expense, to create for itself immeasurable wealth. This state existed in a chronic state of war. Just as the temples were not just religion or mere ostentatious waste, but the very

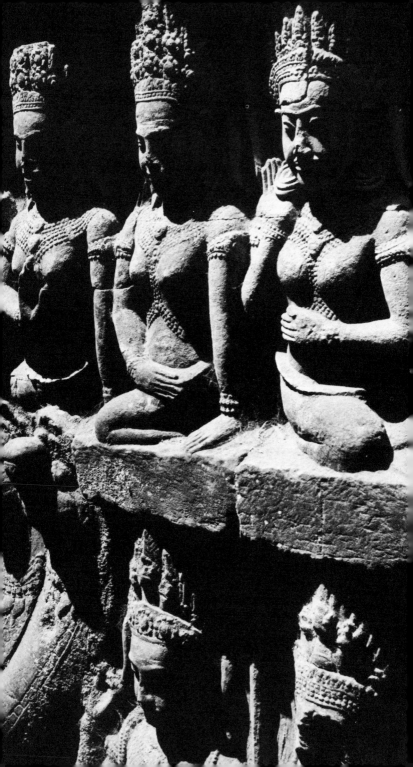

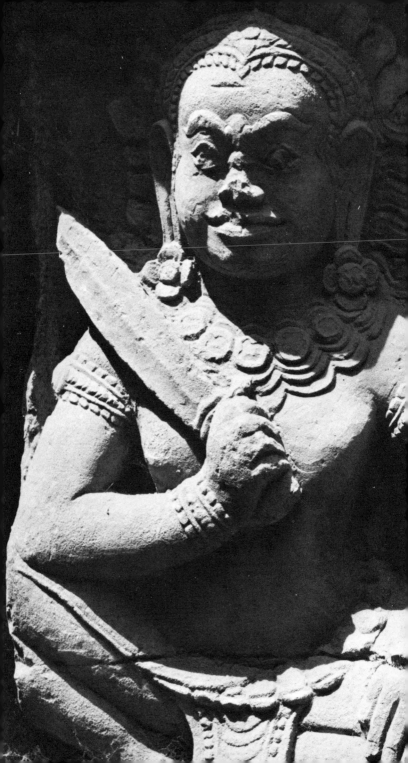

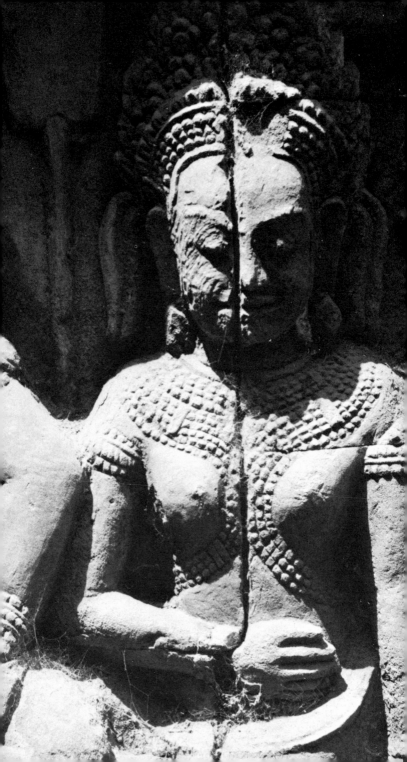

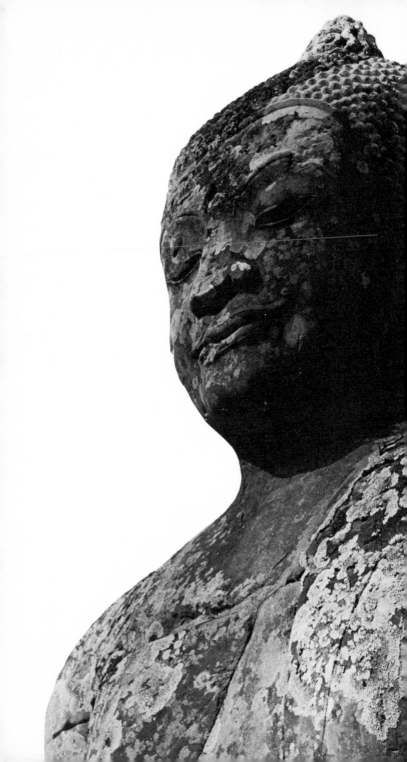

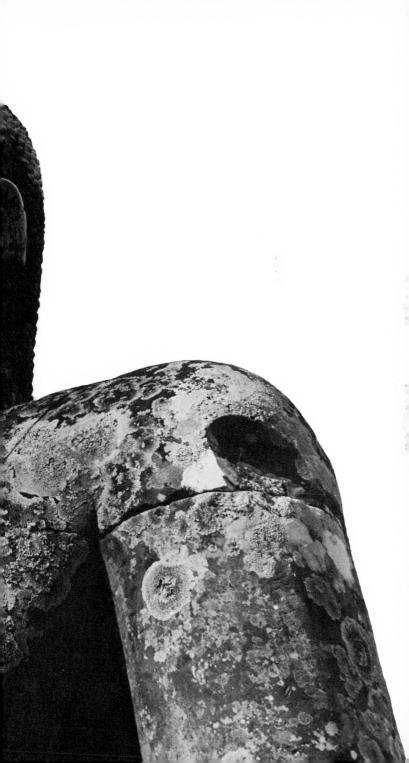

mechanism by which the oligarchy could absorb the people's labor, so these wars were an inevitable form in which the state's organization could exist.

The most comprehensive building period in Angkor's history coincided with—and was an expression of—the inner crisis which shook the state.

No. Not the "agitators," not the buildings, not the war. We must look elsewhere for the key to Angkor's fall.

The King of Angkor was lord of the soil. The oligarchy ruled over the irrigation system. The kingdom was not crushed by a "foreign people," or by a "migration," or by "racial strife." Those who laid waste to the kingdom were "free men" in the same sense that the Germanic tribes consisted of "free men" in contradistinction to Roman citizens. But with Angkor as with the Roman Empire, the internal contradictions tore the state asunder.

One could also say that the tremendous growth in the power and grandeur of the state under Jayavarman VII followed the same pattern as the Roman dominion during the dissolution of the slave economy, or as the European absolute monarchy during the dissolution of feudalism, or as the corporative state is following today.

It was the state of Angkor which was dissolved in the period after Jayavarman VII. In an inscription from 1357 it is said that 139 years earlier (i.e., 1218) was the decisive date:

> From that year, the nobles and the high dignitaries, the Brahmins and the wealthy merchants gradually ceased to occupy the first place in society; also from that time, astrologers and physicians lost their prestige; from that time on they were no longer respected.

This social collapse—the collapse of intensive irrigational agriculture (thus of the centralized state)—was a liberation.

After the fall of Angkor the population changed not only its religion, but also its property laws. Under the law which then prevailed until the French introduced private land-ownership, a farmer held his land feudally. Land could not be sold. It could only be tilled. The result was a more extensive type of agriculture. The farmers became freer. Their taxes were lightened. Slavery changed its form and content.

The new religion—which demanded no huge stone temples—mirrored these new social conditions.

The fall of Angkor was as great a step forward as the fall of Rome, or as the tricolor flying over Paris.

Cambodia has a history of its own. A specific history. It is not "Indochinese" history. This history follows the same laws as the history of Europe. There is nothing "mysterious," nothing enigmatic, about what happened at Angkor.

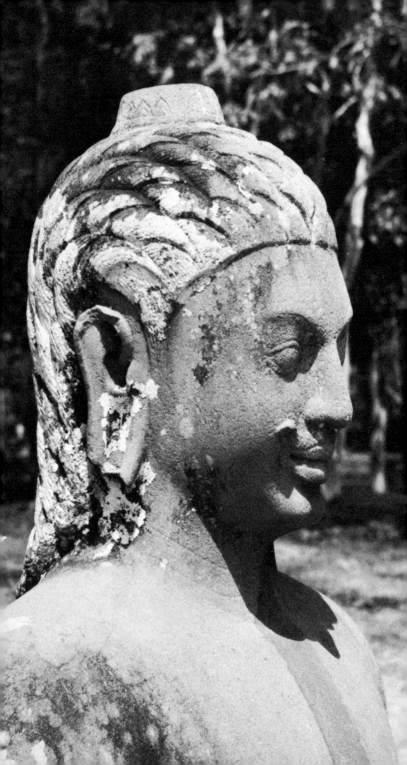

The "Leper"

This sculpture, long known as "the Leper King," stands up on what was probably the royal cremation terrace. It would appear to represent Dharmaraja, the judge of the dead.

Of Angkor only temples remain. The temples were made of brick and stone. All else has vanished. Palaces, hospitals, huts, all were of timber, and have moldered away. No longer is the Chinese silk to be seen at Angkor Vat. The paintings have vanished. Gods of gold and silver have been melted down.

The more powerful Angkor became, the vaster became its stone buildings. When all the good sandstone was exhausted, they built in dark laterite. Its monuments, screened by vegetation, disrupted by the roots of trees, were reconstructed by archaeologists. But Angkor itself was not rebuilt. Only its skeleton.

Before Angkor, men built in timber. After Angkor, they built in timber. Angkor was exceptional. Yet everything in its forms points back to timber architecture. Even its largest temples are only outsize village temples. Nor were the temples of Angkor symbols for some god or other, or some abstract idea. They were power; they were Angkor.

All aesthetic problems connected with Angkor are wrongly put, unless this is borne in mind. Prayers and ceremonies. Sacred texts and learned men. All were merely the form in which the rice crop was collected from the peasants and distributed among the rulers.

These temples are not symmetrical. Nor are they rectangular. But the canals were straight. Power was acquainted with symmetry, and knew how to exploit it, but had itself no use for it.

The construction of these immense temples was conditional upon the majority of the people being called brute beasts.

In the night, when Gun slept and the fan squealed, I thought of Manhattan. Of Paris. And London. Walk down these streets a thousand years from now. How much will remain?